The Argentine Republic
1516-1971

NATIONAL ECONOMIC HISTORIES
General Editor W. E. Minchinton

IN PREPARATION

Hungary: A Century of Economic Development
by I. T. Berend and G. J. Ranki

Poland by M. Malowist

Norway by F. Hodne

France by G. Holmes and P. Guillaume

NATIONAL ECONOMIC HISTORIES

THE ARGENTINE REPUBLIC
1516-1971

✷

H. S. FERNS

DAVID & CHARLES: NEWTON ABBOT
BARNES & NOBLE BOOKS: NEW YORK
(a division of Harper & Row Publishers, Inc.)

This edition first published in 1973
in Great Britain by
David & Charles (Holdings) Limited
Newton Abbot Devon
in the U.S.A. by
Harper & Row Publishers, Inc.
Barnes & Noble Import Division
0 7153 6204 6 (*Great Britain*)
06 492072 0 (*United States*)

Printed in Great Britain by
Latimer Trend & Company Ltd Plymouth

Contents

Tables

8

Foreword

The purpose of this book is to identify the principal stages in the development of the Argentine economy from colonial times to the year 1971. The act of writing a history involves inevitably the use of the historian's own conceptions of what is important and worthy of notice and what is not. The best one can do in the circumstances is to declare one's preferences and say what ideas have guided one in the selection of the data constituting the substance of the narrative. It is the author's belief that the source of satisfactions in the form of goods and services is work, ie the expenditure of human energy and ingenuity. While work is personal and individual, effective, productive work involves specialisation of tasks and social co-operation. To this end men and women have invented social devices such as trade, money, accounting, banking and the investment of capital.

Economic history is an account of how men and women increase their power to work by the invention and development of tools, and how they increase their capacity for co-operation by the invention and development of social devices which enable them to specialise and perfect their individual skills. While economic history suggests that men do tend to improve their capacity to work and to co-operate and hence to produce more and more, there is no reason in principle why the opposite should not happen, and the evidence suggests that it can happen.

Social and political history, as distinct from economic history, suggest that the disposition to work and to improve the power to work, to co-operate and to improve the means of co-operation are not general and universal propensities. Men and women can employ their ingenuity and energy in seeking to

9

live without working at productive tasks, and they often succeed. There is indeed a disposition to regard productive work as contemptible, undignified and unworthy of men and women aspiring to a civilised condition.

These are the simple notions which have served the author in seeking to find a way through the maze of economic data generated by the Argentine community. On the whole they have seemed to serve their purpose, but this is a matter of which readers must judge.

I wish to acknowledge gratefully the assistance given to me by the University of Birmingham and the University Grants Committee which enabled me to visit Argentina; by the Universidad Nacional de Córdoba which accommodated me there and enabled me to use its library and meet some of its teachers and students; by the Instituto Torcuato di Tella of Buenos Aires which opened its doors with customary generosity; and by the Research Department of the Bank of London and South America in London whose members and whose archives are a rich store of information. A list of the Argentines who have supplied me with information, illuminated my ignorance and challenged my ideas would be a very long one. I am grateful to them.

I wish to acknowledge here the kindness and hospitality of two friends: Dr Alberto Moreno and Zulma Pagliari de Moreno.

Finally I am grateful indeed to Miss Marjorie Davies for her patience with a difficult manuscript and its author.

H. S. FERNS

1

The colonial economy

The Argentine Republic is a political community numbering approximately 23,000,000 people who inhabit a territory of 2,777,815 square kilometres in the south-eastern part of the South American continent. It is bounded on the west and north by the high range of the Andes mountains, on the north and east by branches of the vast rivers of the Plata-Paraná system and on the east by the Atlantic Ocean. Argentina has only a small southern boundary with Chile along the Río Gallegos and it shares with Chile the island of Tierra del Fuego at the tip of South America. It lies mainly within the temperate zone, only a small part of the extreme north being within the tropics. Its extreme south touches the 55° of south latitude. Remote though Argentina may seem on the map from the heavily populated areas of the world in Europe, around the Mediterranean, along the coasts and islands of Asia and in North America, the Atlantic Ocean has afforded an easy connection with the great communities around the world. The resources of Argentina are abundant in some categories and relatively scarce in others. Rich land made productive with comparatively little effort has rendered food and animal products abundant, whereas a scarcity of resources such as coal and some of the industrially important minerals has helped to determine the direction and character of productive activity. Any arrangement of human affairs which permits great specialisation of productive activities among the centres of world population through the means of international trade benefits Argentina. Natural or man-made obstacles to specialisation create difficulties for the Argentine

11

people. Free, unimpeded intercourse is much to their advantage. This has been so throughout Argentine history, and is so today.

The Argentina we know had its origins in the Spanish Empire. This empire was an artificial creation of conquerors come from Europe to exploit for their own benefit the people and resources of the Americas. The institutions of Spain and the political needs of their masters determined the character and activity of the empire overseas. From first to last the Spanish dominions in the Americas were controlled with the object of providing an income for the leading institution of Spain, the Crown of Castile. For five-sixths of Spanish imperial history the interest of the Crown was conceived of narrowly in terms of the royal share in the mining of silver and of the taxes on trade goods bought and sold within the framework of an economy devoted principally to the production of one commodity—silver. This activity took place in Mexico and at Potosí in the *cordillera* of what is now Bolivia. The first development of productive and commercial activities in what is now Argentina was connected with the mining industry of what was then the Viceroyalty of Peru.

The silver mines of colonial times were located in a high, barren area which lacked almost everything required by the industry. The Spanish settlements in the foothills of what is now north-western Argentina supplied food, textiles, leather goods, mules, tools and other necessities to the mines.

The colonial cities, Córdoba, Tucumán, San Salvador de Jujuy, Santiago del Estero, Salta and even the more distant city of Mendoza grew up in response to the opportunities afforded by the mining industry, whereas the communities down on the coast, Nuestra Señora de los Buenos Aires and Rosario de Santa Fe, languished. Indeed, such was Spanish economic policy that a customs barrier at Córdoba was established early in the seventeenth century to impede the flow of the few goods which might come in by way of Buenos Aires and the sea.

Thus during the sixteenth, seventeenth and the first half of the eighteenth centuries the area which is now Argentina presented a very different economic character from what we see today or from what has been observed there for nearly two centuries. In the cities of the interior, up against the great mountains and among them, Spanish civilisation flourished with its churches, convents, and universities, nourished by handicraft industry, plantations and ranches and linked together by a commerce moving in carts and pack trains from the foothills to the high deserts where the Indians laboured in the mines. The great plains stretching to the Atlantic coast, where today vast quantities of food and raw materials are produced, were deserts, and the city, Buenos Aires, now the sixth largest in the world, was a mean village having little other purpose than guard-post at the back door of an imperial province whose entrance was on the Pacific Ocean and whose capital was Lima.

The poverty and backwardness of the Spanish settlements by the sea on the shores of the river Plate were not alone the product of arrangements designed to serve the Spanish Crown. The pampas lacked fuel, building materials, men capable of labouring at civilised tasks, and resources readily usable and marketable by Europeans. Unwittingly, however, the Spaniards supplied this last want. They brought horses and cattle to the pampas. These flourished in a wild but benign environment. By the end of the sixteenth century the Indians of the plains had discovered and learned how to use a new food supply and means of movement. The Spaniards had discovered in cattle and horses marketable products—at first hides, hooves and bones— and eventually dried, salted meat, suitable food for men slaving on plantations in the tropics.

As export staples, hides and salted meat had a protean character which transformed the society and political structures of the Spanish Empire in this part of the world and constituted the formative agent in the establishment of the Argentine community as it existed until World War II. At first, in the sixteenth century, the few Spaniards living on the banks of the great rivers found in the wild cattle and horses simply an addition to their food supplies and the means of clothing themselves. In this they differed not at all from the Indians. Once, however, the possibilities were discovered of hides as a commodity marketable across the sea and, thus, as a source of wealth, problems of control and management emerged which ended in the establishment of the great *estancias* under private ownership, the destruction of the Indians and the transformation of the free Spanish and mestizo gauchos into hired cowboys. It ended, too, in the predominance of the ranchers over the merchants as the socially and politically strongest element in the community capable of determining policy domestically and internationally.

The problem of control was rooted in the fact that the killing of cattle and horses cannot go beyond a certain point without threatening the herds with extinction. History affords many examples of the consequences of uncontrolled exploitation of animal and vegetable resources leading to the extinction both of the resources and of the human systems built upon them: the moa of New Zealand, the fur-bearing animals and buffalo of North America, the cereal lands of Mediterranean Africa and Asia Minor. This did not happen on the pampas of Argentina. Early in the seventeenth century the public authorities of Buenos Aires embarked upon an effort to control the slaughter of cattle and to preserve this major resource. Control developed along four lines: the establishment of *estancias* (ranches) in the hands of individuals and families; the establishment of control over labour resources through a system of passports which enabled gauchos to move about only if showing evidence of employment; the registration of cattle brands by *estancieros* and the outlawing of the sale of unbranded hides; and the establishment of a frontier force of policemen-soldiers whose main task was to drive the Indians beyond the ranching areas.

These controls were not established at one and the same time. As late as 1801 Felix de Azara, a Spanish officer, civil servant and naturalist, felt obliged to advocate ranching on the basis of private enterprise as the key to conserving and increasing the wealth in cattle. Whatever may have been the setbacks in public policy and however ineffective the controls may have been at times, the fact remains that the production of cattle products for export increased during the eighteenth century from an estimated 75,000 hides annually during the first quarter of the century to an estimated 1,400,000 hides in 1783.[1] The dangers to the stock of cattle were still there but the institutional bases of conservation and reproduction were sufficiently well established to ensure cattle-raising as an ongoing process for the production of wealth within the framework of a division of labour of world-wide dimensions.

The colonial cattle industry was, of course, modest in size, measured in terms of numbers of establishments and manpower employed. In late colonial times there were only 327 land-owners in the jurisdiction of Buenos Aires and of these only 141 lived outside the city. Azara estimated that an *estancia* required a *capataz* (or boss) and ten men to handle 10,000 cattle. If this was so we can conclude that the labour force on organised privately controlled ranches was small, and that each million hides exported represented the work of only 3,000 ranch hands and 300 overseers. How many more men were required to work the meat drying and salting establishments (*saladeros*) we do not know, but the number cannot have been large. Azara supposed that 30 *saladeros* would employ 1,000 men. These figures, impressionistic as they are, give us a notion, however, of the extensive nature and low labour-intensity of the colonial cattle industry, compared with the mature cattle industry as it existed in the last days of its glory in the late 1930s (1937) when 24,668 breeders and 6,433 fatteners constituted the cattle industry of Argentina[2] and to which was added the major, urbanised meat-packing industry.

Even in colonial times there was an economic feature of the industry which was a compulsive factor in shaping Argentine development until well into the twentieth century. This was the profitability of the industry. Azara observed in 1801 that wealth —measured in terms of money—produced by one man in the cattle industry was approximately three times that of a man engaged in cereal production, and that 10,000,000 cattle yielded greater returns than the silver-mining industry. It is not surprising, therefore, that the cattle industry became the major factor in Argentine economic development and cattle men the most powerful element in Argentine life.

But this is to anticipate. The economy of the Viceroyalty of the Río de la Plata from its establishment in 1776 until its dissolution by revolution after 1810 can be described as balanced, in that none of the several elements in it predominated. Indeed, the cattle industry whose comparative advantages have been described occupied a secondary position in the order of society. *Hacendados* (or landowners) were regarded as socially inferior to merchants and the occupants of public offices, nor did they have a voice in the making of economic policy. This was made in Spain, as it always had been, and it served the interests of the Spanish Crown and the mercantile communities, both Spanish and foreign, which were associated with the Crown. But the establishment of a Viceroyalty with its capital in Buenos Aires and including within its jurisdiction the mining areas of what is now Bolivia was an expression of a determination on the part of the sovereign, Charles III, to enlarge the conceptions and broaden the bases of Spanish economic life. Compared with the economic practices of the Habsburgs, the Bourbon monarchs were men of enlightenment and liberality determined to increase the flow of goods and services within the Spanish dominions. After 1778 merchants in Buenos Aires could trade freely with the major ports in Spain, in the Indies and in the Philippine Islands, and the restrictions upon transactions designed to deliver monopolistic advantages into the hands of mercantile interests in favoured cities of Spain were much diminished so that markets were freer and trade less heavily burdened.

The establishment of the Viceroyalty may have created a balanced economy, but it was a dynamic balance which shifted the growing points of the economy from the interior of the country to the Litoral, the region of the great rivers, and to the city of Buenos Aires. By 1810 Buenos Aires was much the largest concentration of people in the territory of what is now Argentina. The estimated population in 1809 of that territory, exclusive of Indians living in tribal societies outside the Spanish jurisdiction, was slightly over 400,000. Of these 92,000 lived in the province of Buenos Aires, with over 40,000 in the city of Buenos Aires and another 5,500 in settlements like San Isidro, Quilmes and Ensenada close to the city. By comparison the old cities of the interior were modest provincial towns: Mendoza, 7,500; Córdoba, 7,500; Catamarca, 6,500; San Juan, 6,500 and Tucumán, 4,000. The growth of both the city and province of Buenos Aires under the Viceroyalty was an earnest of the pattern of development in the future.

But the future was not entirely present in the condition of the community at the beginning of the nineteenth century. Colonial society was still strongly Spanish and there was present a Negro element which did not persist and which is not present in modern Argentina. Comadrán Ruiz, the foremost student of colonial demography, estimated that in 1804 there were only 475 'foreigners' in Buenos Aires of whom 250 were Portuguese and 108 Italians. Natives of Europe, who were to play a considerable role in Argentine life, were hardly present: only fifteen English, eight Irish, one German and one Scot. North Americans numbered twenty-nine.

Nor was the future entirely present in respect of the structure of the economy. The 'free trade' established by the Bourbons was free trade within the Spanish Empire. Determination to reduce the part of foreigners in this trade—particularly the part of the English, Dutch and French—was stronger and better implemented than it had been under the Habsburgs and at any time until the Seven Years' War. The expulsion of the Portuguese from the eastern bank of the river Plate, the occupation of Colonia and the establishment of a military strong point at Montevideo reduced, if it did not altogether eliminate, contraband trade. Behind the protective barrier of Spanish neo-mercantilism both agriculture and local industries such as milling, woollen and cotton spinning, weaving and dyeing, wood and leather working, salt and sugar refining, viticulture and wagon-building flourished. The industries of Spain competed, but distance and local advantages were serious factors in preserving the viability of local production and arresting the propensity to specialise within the wider framework of a truly international and intercontinental commercial system. Cloths from Upper Peru and Tucumán had still a place in the growing market of Buenos Aires; so had the wines of Mendoza, and the flour produced in Buenos Aires could still be sold there. This was the meaning of balance on the eve of the great revolutionary upset which began to take effect as Spain became increasingly engulfed in the wars of the French Revolution.

The inter-regional commerce of the colonial community in the days of the Viceroyalty depended upon wagon transport

across the pampas and through the mountain passes. In spite of
the great rivers of the region flowing out of a vast tract of the
continent, river transport was not a dominant factor in the
internal movement of goods and the provision of services. Ox-
drawn wagons moved at a speed of 20–21 miles a day over the
rastrillados or trails of the pampas carrying a payload of somewhat more than a ton plus about 1,200 pounds of water, fire-
wood, repair parts and lubricants. River vessels, coastal and
sea-going ships were constructed in Paraguay where the forests
supplied the building materials. In the 1790s residents of Buenos
Aires were permitted to build, own and load their own vessels
for trading in slaves outside the Spanish dominions and for
trading generally and directly with peninsular Spain. Thus, by
the end of the eighteenth century the community possessed a
well-developed transport system which, though primitive and
traditional in terms of motive power, was in terms of extent an
effective agency of economic integration. The railways, motor
roads and airlines which were to come are but technological
improvements and extensions of a transport system whose out-
lines were established in colonial times.

There was a feature of economic and social life in the Viceroyalty of the Río de la Plata which tended to distinguish it
from the old Viceroyalties of New Spain and Peru, and which
rendered easier and more natural the transition of the economy
from a closely controlled imperial mercantilism to international
laissez faire capitalism. This feature was the problem of manpower. In the Río de la Plata, and particularly on the pampas,
manpower was scarce for the purpose of building a civilised
society on the Spanish pattern. The Indians were hard to catch
and hard to keep. The *encomienda* and *mita* systems of labour re-
cruitment, by which the Spanish conquerors of Mexico and
Peru were able to find the means of exploiting people and resources, never flourished on the great plains of Argentina for the
simple reason that the plains Indians could not be put to work.
Quite the contrary. Their adaptation to the use of cattle and
horses enabled them to challenge the Spaniards, to free themselves and to share with the white men the exploitation of the
plains both as a living space and as a commercial resource.

Although the Indians were forced bit by bit to retreat from the pampas of Buenos Aires, it was not until the *salidas de Roca* in the late 1870s that the Indian power was completely destroyed. The pushing-back process yielded few Indians as additions to the labour force at any time on the pampas. The importation of slaves from Africa was attempted. The Treaty of Utrecht accorded to the English South Sea Company the right to establish a factory in Buenos Aires for the importation of slaves, and in the very last days of the Viceroyalty special trading privileges were accorded to the importers of slaves. But slavery as a means of building up a labour force had only a limited success on the pampas. In Catamarca and Tucumán in the interior of the Viceroyalty Africans exceeded 50 per cent of the small population, but in Buenos Aires they constituted only 24 per cent in 1778, and the majority of these were free men. Slaves performed domestic services and worked in various trades like baking and brewing and fetching and carrying jobs, but nowhere was gang slavery established as a basic element in the economy as it was in Brazil, Cuba and the southern colonies and states of North America.

The reason for this is the same as that which enabled the Indians to survive and escape enserfment: the abundance of resources in an environment which made it relatively easy for any man to acquire the means of movement and to utilise that means to escape from the burden of daily labour as a slave, a serf or a wage labourer. The plains and the horses and the cattle made men free in a basic sense. The situation of those who did not choose freedom was rendered different from similar people who lived where only the man of unusual vigour and intelligence or a talent for crime could move up or out of society. As we have already noticed, the major industry of the pampas, ranching, was not manpower-intensive as were the industries of the interior, mining and handicrafts. At the same time development in this or in other industries demanded a larger, more diversified and more skilled labour force. In the days of the Viceroyalty this problem was discerned, but only partially solved.

If ranching was not labour-intensive, it was different from other industries in another important respect. It did not in the first stages of its development require large outlays of capital by the *estancieros* themselves. The mine operator, the miller, the vigneron and even the handicrafts men were obliged to possess a stock of tools and an inventory of raw materials and to hold stocks and wait for payments. For the *estanciero* these requirements were not so restricting. His capital was his herds, and his possession of them depended on the degree to which the state through its regulation of herds, the movement of labour and its defence against Indians could reinforce the *estanciero*'s own efforts in these fields. In the cattle industry capital was accumulated by circumstances or by decisions about slaughtering (which were an expression of income preference). A good example was afforded after the end of the colonial period during the war between Argentina and Brazil, 1825–8. The blockade of Buenos Aires and the interruption of the hide and jerked meat trade caused a great increase in herds, and the investment of cash surpluses in land. Revolutionary war or breakdowns of public order, on the other hand, diminished the stocks of cattle in the hands of ranchers.

In a society in which cattle played so large a part, the socio-economic arrangements leading to capital accumulation and to the financing of production for large markets with long spans of time and place between production and consumption were relatively simple. A silver coinage minted by the state provided a medium of exchange and a measure of value. The *pagarés* (or IOUs) of merchants were almost the sole form of credit. Interest rates of loans were legally fixed at 6 per cent for unsecured loans and at 5 per cent on mortgages. Inasmuch as Spanish merchants had the best connections in the markets overseas in Spain and the other parts of the empire, these merchants were able to finance the largest transactions, ie to supply the immediate cash requirements of producers supplying the export trade. After the outbreak of the French Revolution with the consequent political disturbances to settled patterns of trade, commerce became increasingly speculative with the result that buying and selling in the export trades tended to become divorced from the physical handling of goods. In this way the economic importance of capital, separated from industrial and commercial processes, began to be noticed and its implications in terms of investment better understood.

This noticing of the implications of economic policies and arrangements was, indeed, a feature of late colonial society on the shores of the river Plate. The revolutionary pamphleteer, Mariano Moreno, is well known for his pungent assertion of the principles of *laissez faire* economics on behalf of the landowners of Buenos Aires. This liberal militancy was but the end product and the most pointed expression of much economic theorising during the last two decades of the eighteenth century and the first decade of the nineteenth. The Crown itself and the viceroys were determined proponents of economic development, and the purpose of establishing the office of intendant was to promote economic development. The official interest in development was based on the assumption that the state was the true agency of economic growth. This assumption came increasingly to be challenged by a number of creole writers, of whom the most notable were Juan Hipólito Veytes, Manuel Jose de Lavardén and Manuel Belgrano, later a revolutionary leader and soldier. These were men of ideas as well as active participants in economic and official life. Their ideas differed in certain particulars of principle and emphasis, but they had common themes: the need for world-wide markets and free trade; the need to strengthen the institution of private property as a basis of independent self-interested decision-making; the need to recognise work as the true source of wealth; and the need for improved education and technical instruction. All of them insisted on the development of agriculture and industry as essential to economic development, thus shifting the emphasis from bullion and its production and possession, which was not yet a dead part of the conventional economic wisdom of the Spaniards.

Notes to this chapter are on p 192

2

From the Revolution to Rosas

The political events stretching over more than a quarter of a century, which were part of or flowed from the French Revolution, profoundly affected the Spanish Empire, and in the end so shook it that its political structure was destroyed by revolution. The effects of this revolution upon the economy were nowhere more sweeping than in the Viceroyalty of the Río de la Plata. As a political entity the Viceroyalty was broken apart so that the mining areas in what is now Bolivia were separated from its economic hinterland, and the mining industry was destroyed. Paraguay, with its plantations of *yerba maté*, separated from the communities further down the Río Paraguay and cut itself off, not just from the world overseas, but from its neighbours. The ranching country on the east bank of the river Plate fell under the control of the Brazilian government and, after a bitter endeavour on the part of the government in Buenos Aires to assist in its liberation, became an independent state under the name of Uruguay. The cities and their hinterlands of that part of the Viceroyalty which is now Argentina did not become separate states as did Bolivia, Paraguay and Uruguay, but their political and economic relations with one another loosened to such a degree that they had no common government except in the matter of foreign relations. This looseness of political relations was a reflection of, and a factor in, the break-up of the integrated economy of the Viceroyalty, and an index of a degree of intensified regional self-sufficiency based on ranching, agriculture and town handicrafts.

The revolution in the Viceroyalty of the Río de la Plata cannot, however, be described in terms of political and economic disintegration. On the contrary it involved a new integration into a world-wide complex of commercial activity more open and more all-embracing than that of which the Spanish monarchy had been the controlling agency. Revolution knocked the Spanish merchants out of the system of overseas trading or forced them to establish themselves on a local base. They were replaced by foreign merchants, at first mainly British but not exclusively so. The connection with foreign markets and the sale of foreign goods in Argentina were expanded; or at least the possibility of such an expansion was opened up. The strict Spanish control of foreigners, and the restrictions on their owning property and the obstacles in the way of their lengthy residence stemming from religion and civil law were abandoned by the revolutionary government. Foreigners came to enjoy the same legal rights and economic opportunities as citizens. Old forms of obligatory work service imposed on Indians were done away with. Slavery as a working institution was destroyed. The Inquisition was suppressed and freedom of thought and writing was proclaimed. Customs duties prohibitive of trade were reduced or abolished. The men who made the revolution in the Viceroyalty of the Río de la Plata were in the main liberals with a strong tendency towards *laissez faire* economic and fiscal policy so that, in theory and to a considerable extent in practice, the new state of Argentina, no matter what its constitutional structure, became an early instance of a *laissez faire* economy towards which progressive opinion was working in Europe.

That the Argentine Confederation was not able to impress itself forcibly on the minds of European economists as a model of enlightened principles was due to the comparatively feeble and poverty-stricken condition in which it found itself as a result of fifteen years of strenuous revolutionary effort and confusion. Much capital and manpower had been absorbed in military struggle. Although the revolution was never much in

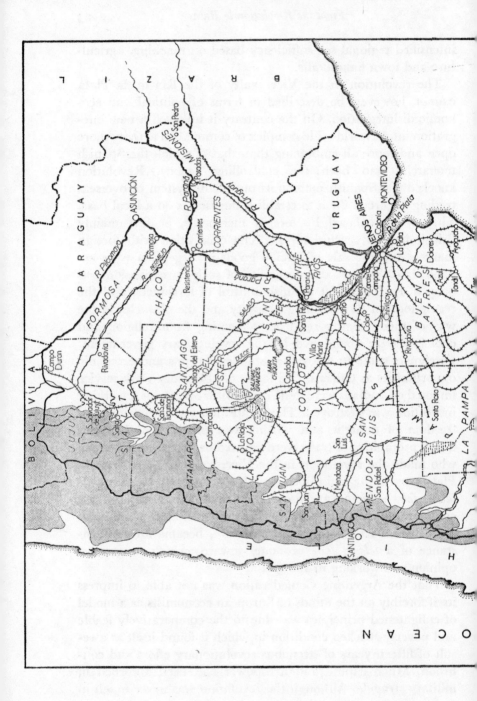

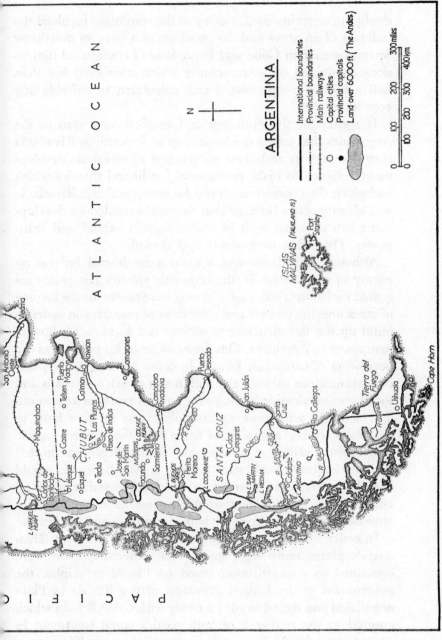

doubt in Argentina itself, victory in the revolution involved the building of an army and the purchase of a navy to overthrow Spanish power in Chile and Peru. War of continental dimensions conducted by a community which numbered less than half a million people was a task calculated to enfeeble any economy.

It speaks for the optimism and revolutionary élan of the Argentines that under the leadership of Bernardino Rivadavia they planned an ambitious programme of economic development designed to make operational the liberal theories which had given direction to much revolutionary activity. Rivadavia and his supporters believed that Argentina needed for development two elements both in scarce supply: capital and manpower. These they proposed to find abroad.

Although Rivadavia was a doctrinaire liberal he was no enemy of state action in the economic sphere. His policy required for its success the use of strong state power for the levying of taxes and the control and allocation of resources in order to build up the infrastructure of society and to attract a flow of manpower to Argentina. One cornerstone of his policy was the borrowing of capital in Europe in order to improve physical communications through the building of canals and roads and social communication through the improvement of education. The second cornerstone of his policy was to give land to colonisers willing and able to bring into the country people from Europe skilled in farming and in handicrafts connected with agriculture. Such state action, it was believed, would stimulate private investment in productive activities of all kinds so that development would become an expanding and autonomous process involving both Argentines and foreigners.

In order to give the foreign interests, so necessary to Rivadavia's plans, more legal guarantees of security than were contained in a constitution based on liberal principles, the government of the United Provinces of the Río de la Plata negotiated and signed in 1824 a treaty with Great Britain which ensured to the nationals of both parties equal treatment in accordance with the laws of their respective states. Thus international law was added to national law as the legal foundation of an international economic and commercial relationship, in which in the 1820s the British were the principal European participants.

The policy of Rivadavia was in its design logical and realistic, and foreshadowed the successful strategy of development of the last half of the nineteenth century. But in the 1820s it was not successful. It required for its implementation political stability, peace and the determined support of at least one predominant element in the community. Although Rivadavia's government was able to market bonds in London worth £1,000,000 at par and from which approximately £570,000 in spending power was realised, and although he was able to induce the establishment of a colony of Scottish immigrants and interest some Germans in a similar enterprise, his plan failed miserably. The Baring loan, so called because it was marketed by this banking house, went quickly into default without any interest or sinking fund charges being paid out of real revenues. The colony, after a good start at Monte Grande in the province of Buenos Aires, was broken up and its inhabitants dispersed. Several British entrepreneurs went bankrupt. The plan as a whole never became operational or permanent.

The first British Consul-General in Buenos Aires had optimistically assured his government of the capacity of Rivadavia's government and the stability of Argentine society. These assurances were soon undone by events. The revolution may have been over, but the political commotions which it had generated were not. In 1826 guerillas crossed from Argentina into Uruguay with the object of overthrowing the authority of the Emperor of Brazil who had established his power there. War broke out between Argentina and Brazil. The guerillas, assisted by an Argentine army, destroyed the Brazilian land forces, and the Brazilians blockaded the river Plate and the port of Buenos Aires. The war had a disastrous and transforming effect on the economy. The treasury was drained of funds to pay for the war. The blockade destroyed trade overseas. Manpower was absorbed into the army. The Indians of the southern pampas, who were themselves considerable traders in hides across the Andes into Chile, took advantage of the Argentine preoccupation elsewhere to press upon the frontiers and break through them.

The immediate effects of the war upon the plans of Rivadavia for developing the economy are obviously easy to explain: less obvious and easy is the identification of some of its other defects relative to the conditions which obtained in the 1820s. His plans not only supposed a peaceful society, but also required for their execution a state apparatus sufficiently well organised to raise the revenues necessary to finance public works and to pay interest and sinking fund charges on capital borrowed at home and abroad. A plan which involved taxing the landlords and had implicit in it a control over the land itself had little appeal to the strongest interest in the country. A plan, too, which involved the introduction of agricultural immigrants into the countryside was not much esteemed by the most numerous and uncontrollable social group, the gauchos. Nor did the plan based upon free international trade find much favour among artisans exploiting the local market for consumer goods. The appeal of Rivadavia's plans could excite the enthusiasm and win the support of those with a sufficiently long view of the community interest, but there was nothing about them either as ideas or as activities which immediately and strongly engaged the interest and support of the men on horseback in the provinces of Buenos Aires, Entre Rios, and Corrientes.

The regime of Rivadavia was undermined by the war with Brazil and destroyed by the civil war in Argentina which followed. Out of this civil war emerged in 1828 the Argentine Confederation, a loose organisation of nearly autonomous provinces. Political fragmentation accentuated regional economic self-sufficiency and obliged the landlocked provinces of the interior to depend more upon localised productive activity and local trade than upon the connection with world markets which revolutionaries like Rivadavia had sought to promote. The economies of the interior provinces tended to stagnate. In Córdoba, for example, the increase in population, which had risen to double the rate of colonial times during the two decades of revolution, fell back to the old rate of the imperial past, and this pause in growth was but an end-product of the brake upon

economic and commercial activity, created by political uncertainty or separatist policies. Such were the economic problems
of the interior provinces like La Rioja, San Juan and Mendoza
that the governments there sought to increase their commercial
relations with Chile. Such also was the unconcern of the government in Buenos Aires that General Rosas, who dominated that
province and represented the Confederation in the international
community, expressed surprise when he learned in 1844 that the
commercial accord between Mendoza and Chile had been
revoked two years previously after lasting for seven years.

In the provinces of the Litoral, however, the connections with
overseas markets were maintained, or at least as much as the
strongest of them, Buenos Aires, would permit to the others:
Santa Fe, Entre Rios and Corrientes. In these provinces the
ranching interests were in control. Their objectives were to sell
as much of their products as they could and to buy what they
needed as cheaply as possible. They were large-scale operators
and enthusiasts for free trade. Trade was as free as the province
of Buenos Aires, controlling the entrance to the great rivers and
the custom houses thereupon, had the political power to allow.

An examination of the records[1] of the maritime customs of
Buenos Aires at the close of the civil war between the unitarian
party of Rivadavia and the federalist party of Juan Manuel
Rosas in the year 1829 will give some idea of the character of
the economy of the province of Buenos Aires and will throw
some light on the economy of Argentina as a whole.

The customs records show in the first place that the balance
of payments for goods imported and goods sold abroad was
seriously in deficit after account is taken of the fact that 15·8 per
cent of exports were gold and silver bullion and plate. The total
value of exports according to the customs returns were 25½
million pesos as against imports valued at 36¾ million pesos. It
is not hard to understand from these figures the inability of the
government to pay interest and sinking fund charges on debts
contracted abroad, or to understand the inflation which had
set in.

The figures for exports reveal both the predominance and the
difficulties of the cattle industry. 77·2 per cent of all exports

were hides, horns, and salted meat, whilst other exports were
very largely the hides, furs and feathers of wild animals. Wool
accounted for less than half of one per cent of exports, and the
only manufactures exported, the product of handicraft labour,
were a few blankets and ponchos made in Córdoba and amounting in value to a tenth of one per cent. The overwhelming reliance was on dry hides, and the total sold abroad, 807,323, was
below the amount being marketed abroad annually during the
early years of the revolution. Of course some allowance has to be
made for the fact that the total exported through Buenos Aires
did not include exports from Entre Rios, Corrientes and Santa
Fe, but it is known that there was very little direct connection
between the river ports and European and North American
ports. The figures indicate the effects of civil war on production,
while at the same time providing a proof of the importance of
the hide trade for the economy as a whole.

The import figures are equally revealing. They show a heavy
reliance on foreign suppliers for manufactured goods. The
products of the machine industries of Britain and France in the
form of cotton, linen and woollen cloths and thread accounted
for 50·4 per cent of the imports, and haberdashery another 9·2
per cent. Surprisingly, Buenos Aires was an importer of food.
Rice, wheat flour, sugar, wine, liquors, coffee, *yerba maté* from
Paraguay and tea from the Orient accounted for 19·2 per cent
of all imports. Iron and ironwork, glass, porcelain, marble and
paint were substantial items, and so were paper and tobacco.
The fact that the maintenance of public authority and military
power had taken a turn in the direction of primitive simplicity
was also reflected in the figures, inasmuch as supplies for the
army and navy accounted for less than 2 per cent of imports, an
expenditure less than that on shoes and furniture.

Shoes and furniture! Wine and sugar! These serve to focus
attention on the controversies over economic policy during the
1830s and 1840s when General Rosas dominated the Argentine
scene. Cattlemen were not the only producers of goods and services in Argentina at this time, and this was particularly so in
the landlocked interior provinces away from the great plains of
the Litoral. Differences of interest and differences of view about

desirable public economic policy were at the root of much of the controversy which the iron hand of General Rosas sought to control. On the one hand there were handicraftsmen in the towns producing shoes, furniture, clothing, ironwork and so on, and in the provinces of the interior there were vignerons and sugar growers seeking markets. International free trade affected these producers. In an attempt to conciliate the interior provinces and local manufacturing interests and to solve the overall economic problem of buying more than was sold in international markets, General Rosas decided upon a protective tariff in 1835. As Rosas said, a poncho made in Argentina cost 30 or 40 per cent more than one imported, but if that was the price of justice to the interior provinces, it had to be paid. The import of a wide range of manufactures of metal was prohibited, and so was the import of wheat and flour so long as prices did not rise above a certain high figure. Duties of 35 and 50 per cent were placed on a wide range of food products, wines and manufactures. Machine-made textiles were not, however, affected. These were in fact the essential raw materials of the handicraftsmen who were being otherwise protected.

The tariff laws of 1835 lasted for seven years. During these years trade was disturbed by a blockade of the river Plate by the French, which was rather better than tariff laws for checking imports. In spite of blockade and protection, local production did not respond to demand sufficiently to prevent large increases in prices, which were further accentuated by monetary inflation. In December 1841 General Rosas quietly took the first big step towards the abandonment of protection when he ordered the removal of the prohibition on the import of a wide range of goods, and within a short time the system of tariffs for revenue, first inaugurated during the revolution and systematised by Rivadavia, was more or less completely restored.

The difficulties of local industry in home markets both in Buenos Aires and in the provinces of the interior at this time were not alone the result of freely admitting the products of Europe and the United States. The revolution and the civil wars had wasted the capital resources of the community. This was especially felt by local business interests because they bore the burden of forced loans, and the subsequent burden of seeing the purchasing power of the obligations of the government wasted by inflation or destroyed by repudiation. Rivadavia had attempted to fund all the debts of the government, to stabilise the currency and to establish a national system of credit through banks. All this had come to nothing. As a result the capital of local businessmen was much reduced and the system of credit reverted to the system of colonial times. Credit was granted by merchants to suppliers of goods which the mercantile houses handled. Quite naturally the merchants could give credit only to those they knew and to those whose products were a security for advances. This meant that ranchers and importers of goods for sale to the public could get credit, and local manufacturers could not. The Casa de Moneda, which Rosas set up in Buenos Aires to handle the issue of money and the accounts of the government, undertook a kind of banking business. It accepted deposits and made loans against readily saleable property, but the Casa de Moneda offered little or no help to small enterprises.

Lack of capital alone does not explain the plight of the small producer. Transport costs along the main routes of trade and travel were high. It was comparatively easy for a European producer to consign goods to agents in Buenos Aires and land them there for sale at what the agent could get for them. Little or no work has been done on the study of comparative freight costs, but enough is known from the observation of merchants to know that a ton of goods moved from Liverpool to Buenos Aires at less cost than from Córdoba to Buenos Aires. This is simple to demonstrate. A ship of the 1830s or 1840s could carry 500 tons, more or less, and took on average 60 days to make the passage from Liverpool to Buenos Aires. Crews of such ships numbered about 25 men. Thus the cost in man-days of moving 500 tons was 1,500 man-days or 3 man-days per ton. The time taken for four men to move one ton 400 miles from Córdoba to Buenos Aires was 20 days. This was a cost in man-days of 80 man-days per ton. Even allowing for wide variations in wages, differences in capital invested per man employed, insurance, port charges and so on, the difference in cost was so great that

Liverpool was in terms of cost much nearer to Buenos Aires than was Córdoba.

Whatever may have been the difficulties of the small producers in towns and the countryside, in the province of Buenos Aires and in the other provinces of the Litoral there can be no doubt that during the regime of General Rosas the big cattlemen did well and the cattle industry grew, improved its productive capacity and extended the range of its productive activities. General Rosas was overthrown in 1852 by another big cattle man from the province of Entre Rios, General Urquiza. A brief examination of the customs records in the last years of Rosas's rule indicates some of the features of the progress made by the cattlemen of which Rosas himself was a leading example.

In 1849 there was a surplus in the balance of trade in commodities. Because of the steady and large inflation of the currency by issues of paper to pay government bills, it is not easy to deduce much from money figures. The volume of goods exported had risen markedly between 1829 and the middle of the century. In 1851, 2,601,140 hides were exported, an increase in 22 years of over 300 per cent. Wool exports increased 2,100 per cent. Salted meat was up 250 per cent; tallow 275 per cent. The Argentine Confederation was paying its way in international markets and was doing so by reason of expansion in its most cost effective sector—the cattle industry.

During the years between 1829 and the overthrow of General Rosas innovation began to manifest itself in the cattle industry. The development of sheep farming and the production of wool and tallow was the most notable addition to production in the pampas. Sheep breeding developed through the introduction of merino stock and European shepherds, many from Ireland. Argentine wool was for the most part coarse and dirty, and it did not compete with Australian wool in the market for fine textile wool. It found its market in the carpet industry in Belgium, the United States and Britain where it was much regarded for the strength of its fibre.

Expansion in hide production was partly due to the extension of the area given over to herds through pushing back the Indians and preventing them from slaughtering for the hide

B

market to which they had entry in Chile. It was due, too, to the more concentrated use of pastures. This was mainly a matter of water supplies. Water was available but its supply in open water-courses was limited, particularly as production spread west and south of Buenos Aires. Wells were required, and lifting water in large enough quantities from the wells was a problem of manpower. This was overcome by the invention of a special kind of bucket made of horsehide stretched over an iron frame and fastened to ropes and pulleys. Although this bucket was hand-operated, its action was semi-automatic, so that approximately two thousand cattle could be watered from a single well.

The semi-wild criollo cattle tended to be small, tough creatures whose meat was hardly distinguishable from their hides. *Estancieros* began to breed for size and flesh during the 1830s and 1840s. Bulls were introduced from Britain for the purpose. This meant closer control of herds. It cannot be said, however, that during the time of General Rosas any startling changes were made. The enclosing of pastures was begun in an effort to control herds. Hedging and ditching were tried with some success, and wire fencing, fastened to metal posts, was introduced, at first to keep cattle out of gardens and then for the purpose of controlling their movement in pastures. Well-digging was itself an assistance in control inasmuch as cattle have generally too much sense to move far from their water supplies.

Growth itself promoted an all-round improvement of opportunities. The number of ships calling at Buenos Aires increased from around two hundred a year in the late 1820s to over five hundred a year in the 1840s. This meant quicker movement to market and shorter periods of warehousing. One advantage of dry hides as a trade good was their comparative durability, but too long in warehouses caused deterioration. This was even more so in the case of salted meat. The availability of shipping space was, thus, itself an aid to improved production.

The expansion of exports was a stimulus to the growth of local industry. A census taken in Buenos Aires shortly after the fall of Rosas showed the presence there of 106 factories and 746 workshops employing 2,000 workers. Inevitably the handicrafts and food trades were predominant, but there were breweries and distilleries, soap factories, carriage-works, metal foundries and sail-makers. Economic growth was likewise a stimulus to immigration. During Rosas's regime the immigrant population grew so that, according to one estimate, a quarter of the population of the province of Buenos Aires was foreign-born. Frenchmen did not begin to migrate to Argentina until the 1830s. By 1854 there were 25,000 Frenchmen, 18,800 British, 4,000 from the United States, 15,000 Italians and 20,000 Spaniards.[2]

What was happening outside the province of Buenos Aires is not well recorded. The history of the economy of the interior provinces has yet to be written. The general impression left by the accounts of provincial life is one of stagnation and difficulty. The province of Córdoba, which is today one of the thriving parts of Argentina, was in the 1830s and 1840s a depressing place from an economic point of view. Political instability, forced loans and the difficulties of transport were severe handicaps. The government of General Manuel Lopez took defensive measures such as levying protective tariffs on goods entering the province, but this kind of policy was no answer to more fundamental social and political difficulties.[3] There is no evidence of immigrants settling in the interior provinces or of any foreign interest in areas so wanting in security to life and property. Even religious orders were not safe. In 1848 the Jesuits were expelled from the province of Córdoba, and those expelled thought it prudent to remove themselves completely from Argentina to the greater security of Bolivia and Chile.[4] Man-made obstacles to trade in the form of provincial tariffs, difficulties of transport and insecurity preventing the accumulation of capital for commercial and industrial purposes combined to retard the communities of the interior, leaving them in many respects worse off than they had ever been in the days of Spanish rule.

Although the post-revolutionary period of Argentina's history until the second half of the nineteenth century exhibited some evidence of economic development, particularly in the provinces of Buenos Aires and Entre Rios, this development was uneven and sporadic, and it did not compare with the phenomenal growth evident in similar areas of the world such as the United States, the Australian colonies, Canada and Brazil.

Notes to this chapter are on p 192

3

A policy for national development

Shortly before General Rosas was overthrown, his minister in the United States, Alvear, endeavoured to persuade him of the need to find methods of modernising the Argentine economy along the lines which were proving so successful in North America. The battle of Caseros in 1852 and the flight of Rosas opened floodgates of discussion, a substantial part of which centred upon plans for economic development. There was wide general agreement among the participants in the debate about the necessity of creating a free-trade area in the nation as a whole by abolishing all inter-provincial tariffs and by removing all obstacles to the movement of goods and people within the boundaries of the republic. There was also wide agreement that free trade meant the right of every province to establish contact with foreign communities through the use of its ports, and that international trade should no longer be channelled through customs houses in Buenos Aires. There was likewise agreement on the need to bring people and capital into the Republic from Europe, and to create the conditions which would induce Europeans to migrate and to invest. A national currency and a banking system were considered objects of national necessity. On the subject of international free trade and participation in a world-wide division of labour, the leading thinkers such as Bartolomé Mitre and Juan B. Alberdi were in agreement. Manuel Fragueiro, a native of Córdoba and the first Minister of Finance in the new national government, had reservations on this subject, and considered that balanced development required protection and state action. In general there was a strong presumption in favour of private ownership of resources. Even Fragueiro, with his Saint-Simonean ideas, was agreed on this point, conceiving of socialism as state action to harmonise interests and to achieve morally desirable social goals. The state itself was conceived of in terms of the dominant liberalism of the mid-nineteenth century, ie a governing institution enforcing laws made by a legislature representative of the community chosen by those presumed capable of rational understanding based on information. Although the state was assigned the important function of making and administering the laws on which all else depended, it was conceived of as a neutral factor which could not and should not undertake economic and social tasks which, with the exception of education, could best be left to private initiative and organisation.

At the centre of the discussion about modernisation and economic development were the questions of labour and capital. It was an undisputed fact that Argentina lacked people. The first reasonably reliable national census taken in 1869 indicated a population of 1,736,923. Estimates made in 1850 and 1860 suggested figures of 935,000 and 1,180,000 respectively.[1] It was widely believed by the articulate people who appeared in public after the overthrow of Rosas that not only were the people few in number, but that these few were not much good for the purposes of economic development. Alberdi argued that a hundred years could be spent on the education of Indians, gauchos and half-breeds and they would still lack the capacity for work of an English labourer. Not everyone took this dark view of their fellow citizens, but there was none the less a belief that manpower supplies must be built up and their capacity for work improved. No serious attention was really given to the potentialities of the mass of Argentines themselves. There was some sense in this point of view, given the facts of the time. The plains Indians were still disputing the possession of the pampas, and as late as 1870 settlers in the southern parts of the province of Córdoba and Buenos Aires found it worthwhile to grow cereals because, unlike cattle and sheep, cereals could not be driven off by the Indians for their own consumption or for sale in Chile. In the end the plains Indians met the same fate as the plains Indians of North America; they were all but exterminated by military action—the *salidas de Roca*—in the 1870s and 1880s. The sedentary Indians and the mestizos of the hills, mountains, valleys and *sabanas* of the interior provinces were an established work force, but it was not until Bialet-Massé's report on the condition of the Argentine working class, made to the national government in 1904, that any serious thought was given to utilising in areas of rapid development the labour supplies lying dormant or nearly so in the less developed parts of the country.[2] Instead, much thought was given to formulating policies which would attract to the country European workers so that Argentina would become, like the United States and the British colonies already were, a place of opportunity sufficiently desirable to induce emigration from Europe.

Just as in the case of importing people, the need to import capital was regarded as a foregone conclusion. Having regard to the circumstances of the 1850s, there were probably no other options open if the object of the community was rapid modernisation and growth. The disequilibrium in levels of economic activity between the Litoral and the interior provinces was a hard fact. The capacity for capital accumulation on a significant scale existed only in the Litoral and particularly in the province of Buenos Aires. If national development, as distinct from regional development, was going to take place, either the resources of the province of Buenos Aires would have to be put at the disposal of the nation as a whole or reliance would have to be placed to a considerable degree upon the supply from foreign sources of the purchasing power needed for railways, public works and machinery. The advocates of development did not explicitly consider the question of capital supplies in these terms, but this was none the less the main item on the agenda of politics.

With so much intellectual agreement about the aims and methods of public policy, it is surprising at first sight that nearly ten years were spent in political dispute before any serious evidence of transformation began to show itself and nearly twenty years before the quantitative evidence of growth became manifest. The notion of national development was attractive enough as an idea, but the attempt to put it into practice foundered at first on the stubborn fact that the province of Buenos Aires was a complex of interests little willing to see their surpluses employed to build railways and finance immigration in remote areas where the lands and resources did not belong to them. This was the essence of the political issue which divided the dominant landed interest.

On the one side was Urquiza, his intellectual mentor Alberdi, and the protagonists of national development. On the other were the politicians, ranchers and businessmen of Buenos Aires. Alberdi devised and Urquiza sought to establish a constitution which placed in the hands of the national government the power to tax and thus to mobilise the financial resources not just of the poor provinces but of the rich province of Buenos Aires. The leaders of Buenos Aires then separated the province from the Argentine state, and attempted to go it alone. This split in the nation persisted until 1861, when under the leadership of Bartolomé Mitre, the forces of Buenos Aires gained the upper hand at the battle of Pavón, and General Urquiza retired from politics.

The separation of Buenos Aires from the rest of the nation between 1852 and 1861 did not altogether destroy the possibility of development. The provinces did not lapse into fragmented anarchy, but under Urquiza's leadership, and with the firm diplomatic support of foreign states, which refused to recognise the province of Buenos Aires as a separate jurisdiction, embarked upon a development programme of their own. The improvement of communications being regarded as fundamental, the government authorised the establishment of a system of post coaches carrying mail and passengers from Rosario to Córdoba, Mendoza, Tucumán and the northern and western provinces. An American engineer was employed to survey the route of a railway to the interior and to estimate its cost. Laws were passed by several of the provincial governments and contracts made for the establishment of agricultural colonies in the provinces of Santa Fe, Entre Rios and Cor-

rientes. In general these contracts authorised entrepreneurs to
bring in settlers, to finance their passage to Argentina and to
establish them on land which the settlers could either rent or
buy. A coloniser or a colonisation company willing to meet the
requirements of the national and provincial governments was
granted tax exemption, and so were the settlers. Settlers were
guaranteed freedom from military service. The colony projected in Corrientes failed because the land selected for the
purpose was remote and of poor quality. In Santa Fe, however,
the landowners, particularly in the central and northern part of
the province where the pastures were still too coarse for really
successful sheep ranching, found in the planting of colonies the
means of realising increasing benefit to themselves by land sales
to colonists and through renting. The Esperanza colony,
founded in 1856, and the San Carlos and San Jeronimo
colonies, founded in 1859, experienced some troubles at first,
largely owing to inadequate capital. They were assisted by the
national government paying off the colonists' debts. Thereafter
these colonies became self-sustaining and by 1864 were reported
to be in flourishing condition. The outbreak of war with Paraguay gave the colonies the stimulus of an expanding market in
Rosario for their cash crops, wheat, barley and oats. The
example of these early colonies converted the landowners of the
central and northern parts of Santa Fe into enthusiasts for
colonisation which found expression in the development of an
active market in land. The same thing happened in the province
of Entre Rios, although on a smaller scale because in Entre
Rios there were certain natural and locational advantages in
cattle.

The national government, operating without the support of
Buenos Aires, thus initiated a process of development which was
a partial success with much promise for the future. Its failures
can be accounted for by a want of financial resources. The railway from Rosario to the interior was planned, but during the
period of Urquiza's government without the province of Buenos
Aires it was impossible to find the capital, amounting to at
least £2.5 million, necessary to build the line.

In the province of Buenos Aires itself attempts at modernisa-

tion and development had some success, and the experience of
these attempts provided guidance in the future. In 1857 the
first Argentine railway commenced operations. The Ferrocarril
Oeste was the work of a group of private entrepreneurs of
Buenos Aires who acquired from the government the right to
build a steam railway from the centre of Buenos Aires to a point
approximately fifteen miles west with the right to build further
west if this was feasible. From the very start the problem of
capital was critical for the promoters. For a time the organisers
of the railway tried to persuade the government that horses
would be an adequate substitute for steam locomotives, and
they employed an argument which has a familiar ring in the
Argentina of today, ie that the capital equipment and fuel
supplies could be locally produced and would thus not affect the
balance of payments. Any government bent on modernisation
could hardly accept this argument, and in the end the proprietors of the Ferrocarril Oeste purchased some rolling stock
left over from the Crimean War: two wide-gauge locomotives
and some carriages and goods wagons. But the problem of
capital remained. In order to prevent failure, the government
invested money. In 1863 it took over the enterprise, and
continued to extend the line so that by 1866 it reached Chivilcoy
nearly 100 miles to the west in the heart of the wool industry.
By this time the railway possessed eleven locomotives, one of
them named 'Going to Chile' (Voy a Chile).

The early experience of the Ferrocarril Oeste demonstrated
that Argentines themselves could build and operate a railway,
but that private entrepreneurs in Argentina lacked either the
capital or the will to undertake enterprises requiring as much
capital and yielding such slow returns as railways. The government had to do the job by employing its taxing power and
credit to draw upon the resources of the community as a whole.
That these resources were adequate in the province of Buenos
Aires was evidenced by the fact of a railway 100 miles in length
built in eight years. That it was an asset to development was
evidenced in the growing traffic moving faster and cheaper than
freight and passengers had ever moved before in Argentine
history. A collateral consequence was a rise in land values as the

benefits of cheaper transport began to manifest themselves in terms of greater profit margins for producers.

Colonisation as a means of attracting people to the province of Buenos Aires was not as straightforward a device as it was in the province of Santa Fe. Most of the good land within reasonable reach of the markets and docks of Buenos Aires had long since passed into the hands of private owners, and even the more remote lands were the domains of men holding thousands of hectares and in some instances dozens or hundreds of square leagues. Colonisation as a government enterprise was only possible in remote areas such as Bahia Blanca then was. Otherwise colonisation was a matter of private initiative, and on the whole in the 1850s and 1860s the landowners of Buenos Aires were not yet persuaded that cereal production, which was associated with colonisation, had a profit potential comparable with wool or cattle production.

The attraction of the province of Buenos Aires for immigrants was not the prospect of farming or owning land, but economic opportunity created by capital investment both in the cattle and wool industry and in the infrastructure, particularly transport. By 1869, the year of the first census, there were 212,000 foreign-born residents of Argentina, of which more than a third were Italians and a sixth Spaniards. It was estimated that 80,000 of the 212,000 present in 1869 had entered the country between 1857 and 1869. The foreign-born were concentrated in the city and province of Buenos Aires and in Santa Fe, Entre Rios and Corrientes, ie the Litoral. In Buenos Aires 30 per cent of the population were foreign-born, and yet in this province land was not easily available except to people with capital. But jobs and business opportunities were, and this was the magnet which drew people from across the sea, and from the interior of the country.[3]

The years between 1852 and 1861 were likewise years of experiment in the field of banking. It was recognised that something better was needed than a system of private credit by merchants and of a finance department of the government such as Rosas's Casa de Moneda had been. The Minister of Finance in the national government of General Urquiza, Fraguiero, proposed the establishment of a national bank with branches in all the main centres of the country. The assets of the bank would be the whole wealth of the country. This wealth could be converted into money available for borrowing, by private persons and for development by the government, in the form of notes. Fraguiero proposed an issue of six million pesos of which one-third would be available for private borrowing, one-third would be available to the government to pay for capital projects such as docks and public buildings, and one-third would be available for government expenses. The entire six million pesos would thus become the circulating medium of the nation. It was pointed out that this was Law's system introduced into Argentina, and that had been a conspicuous failure. Fraguiero's scheme none the less became law. In spite of a determined government effort in the form of paying its bills in 'Fraguiero's paper', the system failed completely and Fraguiero resigned his office, asking history to judge him.

In a sense Fraguiero was a hundred years before his time. In the 1850s in Argentina the only money which anyone seriously trusted was hard money—silver coins of the old Spanish Empire, which still circulated, silver minted in Bolivia, and various European coins. Instruments of credit depended on the individuals whose names they bore, and beyond that on the expectation that these could be converted into hard money. These being the public habits, it is easy to see why the National Bank failed. There was no psychological foundation in experience on which to build. People at large were no more able to believe in its paper than in the issues of General Rosas which had depreciated steadily. Following the failure of the National Bank, Urquiza's government relied on private banking enterprises, the most important of which was the Brazilian Maua Bank.

In the province of Buenos Aires the tendency of thought and practice in the matter of banking was in the direction of semi-private or private institutions. It was recognised in practice that a system based on gold or silver or a combination of both was not feasible in the circumstances which existed in the 1850s. A psychologically credible system might, however, be evolved by separating banks from government as much as possible, and by accepting deposits in either hard money or paper money and undertaking repayment in the money of deposit. The law of 1853 empowered the managers of the Casa de Moneda to pay interest at 5 per cent on deposits, and to exempt deposits from taxes and charges. The next step was to establish a board of directors of the Casa and to change its name to Bank. The directors were appointed by the government, but they were empowered to act autonomously in fixing discount rates and making loans, and they were freed from any obligation to lend money or open a credit for the government unless authorised to do so by the Legislature. By 1860 the Banco y Casa de Moneda of the province of Buenos Aires had deposits of 2,282,000 pesos in hard money and 155,624,800 in paper, and it was an indication of the growing credibility of this approach that as time passed deposits of paper money increased rapidly and deposits of hard money declined.

The experience of banking in the province of Buenos Aires had a marked effect upon the development of national banking policy after the reunification of the nation in 1861. The Banco y Casa de Moneda was renamed the Banco de la Provincia de Buenos Aires, and it became a private bank controlled by its own shareholders and directors. The idea of an all-embracing state bank was rejected and a system of free banking developed in which it was open to private individuals and public authorities to create banks, determine the nature of their services, and seek depositors and borrowers.

Monetary policy was left to the state. Lip service was paid to, and even sincere efforts were made to establish, a national currency based on bullion reserves and managed in accordance with what were considered orthodox European principles. But this was never possible. Argentina lacked a stable currency based on bullion and other saleable assets until 1899. The loose banking laws and the paper currency of Argentina may have been offensive to the contemporary banking mind in London and Paris, but in Argentina itself they proved, on the whole, valuable aids to development in spite of their contribution to speculative booms and almighty collapses. From 1852 until nearly the end of the century Argentina went through the same phase of development in banking as the United States did from the time of Andrew Jackson until the establishment of a national banking system after the Civil War.

It would be incorrect, however, to suppose that easy credit and a paper currency were the essential financial instruments of development. Had this been so the banking system proposed by Fraguiero would have worked and would have been sufficient for the needs of the nation. The stubborn fact is that, given the nature of capital accumulation and investment in the 1850s and 1860s and particularly in the circumstances then obtaining in Argentina, little or no provision for large-scale enterprises such as railways and harbour works would then have taken place under a regime solely of easy credit and paper money. The experience of the Ferrocarril Oeste had demonstrated that private persons were unwilling or unable to finance a large project. Too little was known of capital investment in large and risky projects to attract men to use their surplus wealth other than for investment in tangible assets like land and cattle. Otherwise they held their assets in hard money, and were only beginning to trust deposits in institutions like the Banco de la Provincia de Buenos Aires. The possibility of capital accumulation by state action was equally impossible in the circumstances then obtaining. General Rosas had never been able to finance by taxation alone even the simple tasks of keeping order and fighting Indians and political rivals. He never even tried. He relied on currency issues to make good what he failed to collect otherwise. General Urquiza likewise did not succeed in financing development through the means of a banking system based on paper. The state as an agency of capital accumulation was neither well enough organised nor experienced enough to do what private persons in Argentina were unable to do.

This is why foreign investment was important for development. And this was a very difficult business. Both political propagandists, and, behind them and supplying them with ideas, serious students in Argentina today, have elaborated a myth that wily foreign capitalists, mostly British, saw the possibilities of wealth in Argentina and moved in. The truth is quite otherwise. From 1852 until approximately 1880 it was only with the utmost difficulty and by resort to nearly every trick known to promoters that foreign capitalists could be induced to supply the resources required to build the infrastructure which intelligent people recognised as essential for development.

Europeans possessing wealth over and above their current requirements were very like Argentines of the same condition. They wanted security and they wanted rewards for the use of their wealth. The only way in which a vicar in Norfolk in the 1850s and 1860s differed from an *estanciero* in Chascomus in the matter of using surplus funds consisted in the greater experience of the vicar, or more likely his attorney, in investment in railway companies or in banking enterprises. In spite of frequent failures of enterprises in Britain, a sufficient number of them had actually paid rewards to the vicar and his like for there to exist a belief that buying railway stock or investing in government loans was not actually a means of loss but, on the contrary, a means of gain. In Argentina, on the other hand, a belief of this kind could not yet be founded on experience. Quite the opposite. Two generations of Argentines had had experience of forced loans either repudiated or paid in currency much reduced in purchasing power to that taken for them.

No matter what the experience of European capitalists may have been, Argentina was a remote and largely unknown place of which reports were not reassuring. In England there was the memory of a loan that had failed within a twelvemonth. Frenchmen had observed the British experience, and there was a numerous colony of Frenchmen in Argentina (larger than the British) whose experience of government in Argentina was no different from that of Argentines themselves. The Germans were not yet given to investment outside their own territory, and the Americans were fully occupied developing their own country. The problem of finding investment funds for the financing of an infrastructure of the kind possessed by western Europe, the United States and the British colonies was, therefore, not an easy one.

A key word in the investment process of the 1850s and 1860s was 'confidence'. Confidence simply meant some sort of proof that if the sum A was given to a man or an institution it would be returned to the investor as A plus a fraction of A. If there was confidence based on actual experience, as distinct from talk, that this happened in a fairly high proportion of cases, investment and re-investment became an ongoing process and economic growth a reality. The establishment of this kind of confidence was the work of the government of the province of Buenos Aires during its period of separation from the rest of the nation. It did this by undertaking to repay the loan made to the Argentine government in 1824, and to repay not only the principal but the accumulated interest. It baulked at paying interest on interest, and the representatives of the creditors gave way. As a result Argentine resources began to flow into the pool of capital in Europe, and capital from that pool began to flow to Argentina, thus making possible the payment of wages to men building railways, the purchase of machines, and the operation of plant until such time as the revenues of enterprises could cover current and finally capital costs. In grasping what happened in Argentina in the 1860s two points must be borne in mind. The first is that the Argentine state through its taxing capacity mobilised the resources of the community on a sufficiently large scale to feed capital into the international pool of capital in the form of repayments of principal and interest. At first and up to a point Argentina's drawings from the capital stock of Europe were greater than its payments into that capital stock, and in this way the costs of development were spread beyond the Argentine community, and Argentine resources correspondingly freed for use in projects such as the cattle and sheep industry of which Argentines had the most knowledge and in which they had the most confidence. In this way, too, development was speeded up. The second point which must be grasped is the conditions under which capital in Europe was released for investment in Argentina. No great institution could decide on investment in Argentina. A banking firm like Baring's might recommend Argentine securities and in a sense attach their name to them by offering them for sale, but only the decisions to invest of a large number of comparatively small capitalists could ensure the success of an investment project or a loan. Investment in a large project or a loan to a government was a social enterprise which worked only if a response in the shape of money payments was evoked from the participants. Hence the importance of the action of the government of the province of Buenos Aires in undertaking to repay the loan of 1824.

This undertaking to honour a bond became a cornerstone of Argentine government policy and has remained so down to the present day. Whatever the state of the economy or the currency circulating in Argentina, the government has always endeavoured, and has nearly always succeeded, in honouring its bonds written in terms of a hard currency of its own or in terms of some stable foreign currency. As the role of the state diminished in the investment process and as it became more a matter of private enterprise, the flow of investment came to depend more on capacity to make profits than upon the willingness and ability of the public authorities to honour their bond. But in the beginning the honouring of bonds was extremely important.

The public authorities both national and provincial employed their credit once established in a variety of ways. The first was direct investment in useful works. It has already been noticed how the government of the province of Buenos Aires took over and developed the Ferrocarril Oeste. The national government built and operated the first railway from Córdoba to Tucumán and the north-west. A second device for stimulating capital investment was to guarantee profits on private investment in railways. The Ferrocarril Central from Rosario to Córdoba, first planned in the 1850s, started in 1863 and completed in 1870, was an instance of a guaranteed railway. Guaranteeing profits generally at 7 per cent on a predetermined capital became a common and in the end a much abused system which was finally terminated after the Baring crisis of the 1890s.

The Ferrocarril Central was also an example of another form of subsidy—the land grant. The Central was granted three miles of land each side of the line from Rosario to Córdoba; in all an area of approximately 750,000 acres. Much of this land had to be expropriated by the public authorities and its owners compensated. Land values were low, but once the railway was built they increased rapidly. Land-grant railways were not, however, an easy proposition because most of Argentina, at least in the areas of possible development at that time, was already in private ownership. More often a roundabout system was employed in uninhabited areas. The provincial authorities auctioned off their public lands to pay interest and sinking fund charges on loans which were used to pay railways guarantees and/or subsidies. This system was the delight of land speculators, who bought lands cheaply from the state and watched them appreciate in value as a railway was built and their holdings were brought into use by the work of others.

The important role of the state in the process of development was something which the liberal thinkers had not fully considered. In many respects it ran counter to their philosophy of private property, private initiative and private enterprise, and demonstrated some of the shortcomings of their dogmas. This importance of the state was but a phase. It did not lead on to an increasing domination of the state in the economy. Canada and Australia went through a similar phase. Theirs was businessman's socialism: state action on behalf of private industry. In Argentina it was *estanciero* socialism: state action on behalf of landowners.

It is impossible to relate or explain the history of the Argentine economy during the 1850s and 1860s without making reference to the evolution of the international economy to which Argentine developments were a response. During these years the slow triumph of the modernisers and reformers in Argentina and the slow growth of confidence on the part of European investors had a solid foundation in economic activity itself. The Crimean War had a favourable effect on the sales opportunities of Argentina's well-established trade in hides and wool, and prices rose as well as production. Repaying the English loan of 1824 and establishing a degree of confidence in the investing class was not just a product of political and moral wisdom. It was made possible by increasing production and an increasing flow of funds from sales abroad. A few figures for the decade of the 1850s will illustrate this.

When Argentina was once more united as a single state and market area under the government of General Mitre in 1861 economic circumstances from the Argentine point of view were good. The American Civil War had pushed up prices, and had generated an interest in Argentina on the part of the British as a possible new source of cotton supplies. Wool exports, which had amounted to 12,454 tons in 1855 and 17,316 tons in 1860 reached 54,926 tons in 1865 and 70,230 tons in 1868. The total value of exports was likewise climbing steadily, and so were imports. In spite of this steady growth in the 1860s a crisis developed in 1866. The end of the Civil War in the United States was an important factor for Argentina. The triumph of the North and of the protectionist interests, which were not solely industrial, resulted in a tariff on coarse wool imposed by the US Congress. Argentina supplied 95 per cent of this market. The prohibitive tariff hit Argentina hard. Wool sales in the USA fell from 13,148 tons valued at 3,057,844 pesos in 1865 to 1,972 tons valued at 396,591 pesos in 1868. Prices, too, were affected. Wool in the Buenos Aires market in 1867 was selling at 13 per cent less than in 1865; 15 per cent less in 1868 and 28 per cent less in 1869. The only bright feature for the pastoral interests was the steady rise in the price of hides during these years, but even this favourable factor was somewhat clouded by the fact that the price of hides rose more in Buenos Aires than it did in Hamburg, probably owing to increased local demand on account of the war in Paraguay.[4]

Gloom and demands for action began to develop among the pastoral interests. In 1866 the Sociedad Rural was formed to represent the interests of the cattle and sheep men and to plan policy. At its first meeting its secretary Eduardo Olivera argued :

The Argentine Republic and particularly the province of Buenos Aires, has only one industry which nourishes it and gives life to the entire society. This is the pastoral industry. For some years now the decline of the demand for meat [salted for export] has hit the cattle industry hard, and reduced it to dependence on sheep, which today is threatened with conflicts about the deterioration of breeding stock and by the lack of acceptability of the product. These facts oblige us to pause at the edge of the abyss and ask ourselves where we are going and if there is some means of avoiding the catastrophe which faces us.[5]

Olivera proposed more capital investment and the expansion of the area of production. This was to become the fundamental strategy of Argentine economic policy until world markets began to be restricted after 1929 and until the open British market was restricted by the Ottawa agreements of 1933. Another policy was advocated which did not become part of the Argentine strategy, ie a policy of tariff protection designed to build up industries capable of absorbing pastoral products. A tariff on woollen goods was recommended, and some of the leading members of the Rural Society attempted to organise a woollen textile company. This in turn provoked a more general questioning of the Argentine policy of free trade. Fidel Vicente Lopez, who was both a landlord and a professor of political economy in the University of Buenos Aires, argued that it was a mistake for Argentina to adopt the political organisation of the United States but not its policies of industrial protection. In fact, however, the landed interest of Argentina then and later was no more willing, for economic, political and social reasons, to consider policies of industrial protection than the plantation owners of the old South had been willing to do so before the American Civil War.

Notes to this chapter are on p 192

4

Two decades of development, 1870-1890

From the permanent unification of the Argentine community in 1862 until the seemingly permanent intrusion into Argentine affairs of military officers in 1943, the Argentine economy functioned and developed in response to clearly recognisable economic stimuli. Landowners used land, capitalists invested capital and workers worked in response to opportunities to maximise income. This system worked in the sense that economic development in terms of production and wealth was a consequence. Flows of capital to Argentina and within Argentina were a response to the possibility of profits. Men and women came to Argentina and moved within Argentina in response to opportunities to earn wages, and if these opportunities diminished and/or real wages declined the flows diminished or reversed. Entrepreneurial techniques, management techniques and the use of simple and sophisticated tools for the performance of productive work developed within the framework of the macro-economic relations of the system as a whole. This is the story lasting roughly eighty years: a story of a dynamic equilibrium model in active operation experiencing fluctuations in activity which were the self-corrections of a moving system productive of increasing incomes for the participants.

While it is possible to view the process as a whole over eighty

53

years in these terms, it is convenient for the purposes of comprehension to break down the history of the process chronologically, relating periods of time to changes in the volume and variety of products, the work processes of production and the social relations of the participants in the system as a whole. The period 1870 to 1890 is fixed in time by two facts: that the Ferrocarril Central, a major feature of the infrastructure planned earlier, was completed in 1870, and that in 1890 the Baring crisis terminated a phase of capital investment and immigration. During these two decades certain features of transformation and growth can be discerned which lend themselves both to description and to analysis.

Until 1870 the growth of the Argentine economy meant more of the same: more hides, more wool, more tallow for export. Imports had begun to change: more manufactures of iron and steel, but still more textiles, more food products, more house furnishings and so on. During the years 1870 to 1890 growth in terms of more of the same ceased. Increases in variety as well as volume became a characteristic feature of the economy with important secondary effects upon commercial and social life. Sheep and cattle raising grew substantially, but cereals became established as part of the domestic food supply and as staples of export. Flour milling became an Argentine industry and imports of flour from the United States and elsewhere dwindled. National self-sufficiency in sugar and wine became a possibility. The export of live cattle developed, and the late 1880s saw the foundations being laid of the export of frozen and chilled meat. Industries using heat engines began to develop. Quarrying for building materials was established and grew rapidly. The harvesting of timber for building materials and fuel became important industries. The variety of occupations increased, and the urbanisation of the community was accelerated.

Underpinning the growth of the two decades 1870–90 was railway expansion in Argentina, and the expansion and technological improvement of ocean shipping. During this time the length of railway line multiplied over ten times from 836km to 9,400km. By 1890 only three provinces lacked railways. The growth of the railways is shown in Table 1.[1]

TABLE I

Growth of the Argentine railways, 1870–1890

(length of track in kilometres)

Province	1870	1875	1880	1885	1890
Buenos Aires	326	649	1,070	2,297	3,135
Santa Fe	300	300	300	450	2,266
La Pampa	—	—	—	—	—
Córdoba	200	561	730	889	1,123
Santiago del Estero	—	—	—	191	500
Catamara	—	189	189	189	362
Tucumán	—	—	128	128	361
Salta	—	—	—	—	144
Jujuy	—	—	—	—	—
La Rioja	—	—	—	153	153
Entre Rios	10	115	115	115	412
Corrientes	—	50	50	56	120
San Luis	—	35	35	216	327
Mendoza	—	—	—	243	243
San Juan	—	—	—	84	84
Rio Negro	—	—	—	—	—
Chubut	—	—	—	—	70
Total	836	1,899	2,617	5,011	9,300

Railway building was financed almost entirely by European capital. More than half the railway mileage was owned and operated by foreigners, mainly British. The remainder, financed by public loans abroad, was operated by Argentine public authorities, either the national or the provincial governments. Three different gauges were already in use. By 1890 two British-owned lines, the Ferrocarril Central and the Ferrocarril Sud were arterial systems: the first linking Córdoba with maritime transport at Rosario, the second linking the south and south-eastern pampas with Buenos Aires. The Ferrocarril Oeste, owned by the province of Buenos Aires, performed a similar function for the pampas west of Buenos Aires. The national government had built a line north and west from Córdoba linking Tucumán, Catamarca and Santiago del Estero with the Litoral. The province of Santa Fe built lines north from Rosario and Santa Fe to serve the expanding wheat-growing areas of the central and northern areas of the province. A small system existed in Entre Rios to link the interior of the province to the river port at Paraná.

The Ferrocarril Oeste and the Ferrocarril Sud were profitable systems almost from the moment of their establishment. The Ferrocarril Central required fifteen years before its shareholders ceased to rely on the government guarantee for their dividends, and it was the subject of much complaint by users on account of the deficiencies of its rolling stock. The explanation of the difference between the Ferrocarril Central and the other two related to differences in the calibre of management and differences in the territories served. The Ferrocarril Central ran through less-developed territory than the other two, and was in a certain degree a pioneer railway which depended for its profitability on the use that its construction generated in the countryside through which it passed. But there is evidence, even at this early date, of endeavours to solve problems of profitability not by expansion through competitive pricing but by rate-fixing in collaboration with existing transport interests depending on ox wagons.[2] In the case of the Oeste and Sud an unalloyed resolution to compete by offering cheap service paved the way to success. The Sud never relied on a government guarantee, and soon sought to reduce government control to a minimum. The further is extended its lines, the more it cut into the ox-wagon trade, because the longer the haul the lower the proportionate cost of labour.

In general, the cost of railway building on the pampas was low compared with building in North America, Europe and elsewhere in South America. The government guaranteed a capital of £6,000 per mile in the case of the Ferrocarril Central. This was in the 1860s, and there may well have been substance in the complaints of the proprietors that a capital of £6,000 per mile was inadequate. After 1873, however, the cost of steel rails began to drop from a peak of £15·50 a ton that year to £9·80 a ton in 1874 and to £4·00 a ton in the 1890s. In the 1870s the Sud built extensions for £4,000 per mile, including rolling stock, signalling equipment and stations. In the sierras north and west of Córdoba engineering problems, and hence costs, were greater than on the pampas, and it was here that the government was obliged to build the railways for want of bold risk-taking capitalists willing to build into areas of uncertain market potential and comparatively high costs.

During the 1860s and 1870s there had been much technical improvement and expansion of the world's fleet of sailing and steam ocean-going vessels. The price of ocean freights remained steady until 1877, but then began to decline, and by 1886 ocean freights were 40 per cent down on 1877 and by 1896 were half what they had been twenty years earlier. As a result there was a considerable decline in the proportion of the cost of cereals attributable to transport charges. It is not surprising that Argentine cereals began to enter world markets only two years after ocean freight rates began to fall, and that from 1879 Argentine wheat production was able to expand rapidly in spite of falling prices in world markets.

Hides, wool, tallow and cereals could be shipped abroad as easily in sailing vessels as in steamships. With these commodities, availability and cost were the only matters of concern. Steamships, however, were the technical foundation of shipping live cattle and refrigerated meat. The speed, superior size and certainty of movement of steamships and the various ways in which heat energy could be transformed into the means of refrigeration and ventilation opened up possibilities in the marketing of sheep and cattle that had hitherto not existed. In 1876 a French steamship *La Frigorifique* fitted with an air conditioning system designed to maintain a temperature of 0° C arrived in Buenos Aires with meat killed three months previously in Rouen. The meat was eaten at a banquet. Its badness was insufficient to abate the enthusiasm of those seeking the expansion of the market for cattle. Within two years, however, another French development consisting of deep freezing at temperatures up to − 30° C was exhibited in Buenos Aires, and this represented the technical beginning of the frozen, and later chilled, meat trade.

The development of the physical system of transport was

matched by the growth of a system of financing the operation of the individual units of production: ranches, cereal-growing establishments, marketing organisations and industries serving the needs of producers and consumers. Foreign capitalists played a part in the banking system—the Bank of London and the River Plate, founded, owned and operated by British bankers, was for most of this period the principal bank in the province of Santa Fe, for example—but the banking system as a whole was very largely developed by the Argentines themselves. Although it was the intention of the public authorities to establish banking on what were regarded in Europe and the British dominions and increasingly in the United States as sound principles, the public demand for credit was such that the good intentions of the public authorities were overborne, so that the banking system was a free one, and the system of inspection was unequal to the preservation of ratios of saleable assets to notes and loans which experience had shown to be necessary for a stable system. Banks were founded to do the ordinary business of accepting deposits and lending money for commercial operations on the security of trade goods and the known capacity for repayment of borrowers. Land mortgage banks were also founded to provide long-term credits for landowners. These land mortgage banks provided resources to borrowers, not out of the deposits of the public, but from the sale of land mortgage bonds called *cédulas*. The land mortgage bank issued the bonds to borrowers on the security of land, and the bank took responsibility for the ultimate redemption of the bonds, but the borrower sold the bonds delivered to him on the open market for what he could get for them and he could likewise buy *cédulas* on the open market to discharge his debt. *Cédulas* found their way to Europe, and thus the European investor became in this way the financer of development in the Argentine.

The currency of Argentina during the 1870s and 1880s consisted of bank notes and foreign coins, mostly silver. In 1863 the national government passed a law stating that it would pay its employees in the paper notes of the Banco de la Provincia de Buenos Aires at the gold exchange rate of the day of payment. In this way there began the recognition of two currencies: the paper currency in circulation and the hard currencies of international commerce. In September 1875 President Avellaneda promulgated a law establishing the *peso fuerte*, as distinct from the paper peso, as the national coinage. The *peso fuerte* was declared to be 1⅔ grams of gold nine-tenths fine. There was, however, no means of coining the *peso fuerte* and putting it in circulation. None the less, the *peso fuerte* became a means of measuring the exchange value of the actual paper pesos in circulation, and the means of writing a contract between two or more parties wishing to express a value having some stability over time. In 1881 President Roca endeavoured to establish a bimetallic system with a fixed ratio of 25:1·6129 between silver and gold. Quite apart from the fact that this involved an overvaluation of silver, the system of Roca was no more capable of being established than that of Avellaneda. The gold and silver did not exist in the Banco Nacional nor in the treasury, and there was no interest in the community sufficiently strong to insist on either a gold or a bimetallic standard. Quite the contrary. The major interests—the ranchers and farmers—were enjoying the benefits of a system which tended to reduce real debts and real wages, while receipts from exports were fixed in gold or gold-backed currencies.

The bulk of the revenues of the national government was derived from taxes levied on imports and exports. The provincial governments were, and long continued to be, poor in terms of tax revenue. Taxes on land and on business enterprises were the principal sources of tax revenue. All the provinces possessed public lands, and the sale of these was a source of income during the 1870s and 1880s, but not as great a source as they might have been, inasmuch as no government ever devised a policy which enabled them to sell land after the building of a railway had enhanced its value. Governments both national and provincial limited their taxing capacity in the interest of development by granting tax exemptions to railway companies, to colonists and colonisers, and to business enterprises connected with colonisation.

While the general tenor of Argentine fiscal policy was *laissez faire*, neither the national executive nor the Congress

was pedantically doctrinaire in a belief in liberal policies concerning international trade. To encourage wheat growing and
flour milling, import tariffs were levied on wheat and flour in
1876, and export duties abolished, and these tariffs and exemption from export duties were retained until wheat exports were
well established in the 1890s. Similarly with sugar. Argentine
sugar tariffs led to a trade war with Brazil, and as a consequence
Argentina lost the Brazilian market for cattle and sheep. There
was not much consistency in tariff policy. High protection was
given to the jute bag manufacturers in spite of bags being an
important cost item of the wheat producers. On the other hand,
Argentine producers never had to contend with protective
tariffs on farm machinery and similar manufactured imports
used in ranching and farming.

The opening-up of internal and foreign markets by the development of transport, which was both cheaper and more
versatile than hitherto, brought great changes in ranching and
farming. These changes required heavy investments of capital,
and it is easy to see why Argentine capitalists refused to invest
in railways, public works and secondary industries. Their resources were required to mount an adequate response to the
new opportunities presented to them both at home and abroad.
To respond profitably—to respond at all—to the demand in
Europe for meat, both sheep and cattle had to be bred for meat
instead of for wool and hides. Pastures had to be improved. All
this required investment in breeding stock, fencing, well drilling
and stock handling.

Argentine sheep which produced the wool and tallow of the
1840s, 1850s and 1860s were in general, and in spite of the
existence of some well-bred flocks, a degenerate breed of
merinos. Sheep were required which produced wool, but with
a carcass which carried flesh. Care had to be taken with breeding the race of Lincolns, which experience proved to flourish
best on the pampas, and they had to be pastured on 'soft camps',
ie on pastures where the coarse grasses of the original pampas
had been destroyed and the tender grasses allowed to develop.
They had, too, to be pastured on land with a good carrying
capacity so that the animals did not have to wear themselves

out searching for food. All this meant control and control meant investment.

What was true of sheep was even more true of cattle. The criollo cattle of colonial times were thin, small, hardy creatures whose hide was the best part of the animal commercially. Some improvement had been effected to meet the requirements of the salted beef industry. The development in the 1860s of the beef extract industry based on a vacuum boiling process invented by Baron Liebig (the only successful attempt of many to find ways of processing Argentine meat for a wider market) also increased the demand for better-fleshed beasts. When it became practical to ship live cattle overseas and to market frozen and chilled meat, a wholly new type of animal was required, carefully bred for size and flesh and pastured and finished with care on 'soft camps' not only natural but artificial, ie on alfalfa. This, too, meant big investments of capital in fencing, hedging or ditching pastures and the importing of breeding stock. Wire fencing, Shorthorns, Herefords and Polled Angus became important items in the list of capital goods imported along with rails and locomotives. Specialisation began to develop, too, as between breeders and finishers. Breeders began to locate on cheaper land on the frontiers of settlement, and the finishers and fatteners on land near the ports of embarkation and the centres of local consumption.

The development of a national and international market for cereals required the abandonment of agricultural methods inherited via Spain from the Roman Empire. Given the abundance of land, the cereal farmers quickly abandoned the romantic notion of the colonisers, who thought in terms of planting a race of self-sufficient peasants working away at the production of fruit, poultry, milk, cheese and breadstuffs. As soon as wheat became a big cash crop the Argentine farmer went for extensive cultivation. Once he began to plant large areas, which he could still do by hand, he was obliged to harvest and thresh with machines. Again capital was needed. Long before the modern businessman had discovered the wisdom of renting equipment as a means of economising capital, the Argentine cereal farmer had discovered the advantages of renting. He rented everything:

land and machines. For him the goal was the big crop sold for cash as quickly as possible. The picture of the Argentine farmer as a share-cropping slave without home and without property is a false one. His object was money: to get in and get out, and more often than not he got in with nothing and he got out with something. After the initial effort to establish colonies had spent itself by 1885, the proportion of renting farmers steadily increased, and many owners of small farms themselves rented land from others and to others, so that farmers renting land constituted the majority of Argentine cereal growers.[3]

The expansion of cereal production was at first associated with colonies, which, both in the intention of their founders and in their activity, resembled the small farms which supplied food to provincial cities such as Córdoba. The Paraguayan war, the establishment of the railway from Rosario to Córdoba, and the encouragement given by government tariff policies encouraged expansion in central and northern Santa Fe and southern Córdoba where the planting of colonies was shown to be more profitable to landowners than sheep or cattle. These areas became a specialised wheat zone, and in the first stages of the entry of Argentina into the world wheat market, which dates from 1879, the shift from dependence on imports of wheat and flour to large surpluses for export was a result of this specialisation based on the most profitable use of resources. However, once the overseas markets for live cattle and frozen mutton began to develop from 1885 onward, cattle and sheep producers began to discover a method of converting natural and 'soft' camps to alfalfa fields by renting to cereal farmers on short leases including a contract to sow the land to alfalfa at the end of the lease. Thus the cereal farmers ploughed the camp for the first time, sowed it to cereals for one, two or three years and then planted the new pastures and forage needed for finishing meat animals. As a result of this system of rotation, cereal production was meshed in with cattle and sheep ranching, and cereal production spread into areas hitherto given over exclusively to cattle and sheep: southern Santa Fe Province, south-eastern Córdoba, Entre Rios and the province of Buenos Aires.

Cereal production up to the point of delivering the harvest

was more demanding of manpower than cattle and sheep production up to the same point. Ploughing and sowing required manpower which the farmer, his family and a comparatively few hired hands could supply. Harvesting and threshing demanded much labour for a short period of time. High wages had to be paid to attract seasonal labour. Although figures are not available for the 1870s and 1880s, the studies of wages made by the Argentine Ministry of Agriculture at the end of the century showed that wages paid to seasonal workers of varying grades of skill and responsibility were from three to six times those paid to farm workers paid monthly for ploughing and sowing.[4] In addition to money wages, harvest workers received food and lodging, so that wages represented a net sum which the worker could accumulate or gamble away and spend as he chose. There developed a movement of seasonal workers to and from Spain and Italy known as *golondrinas* or swallows. But it must also be noted that these workers were paid in paper currency, and the gold premium had a marked effect on this source of labour.

Whatever the advantages to the farmer of paper currency in reducing the cash wage bills, these were only of a short-run kind. His permanent solution to labour shortage and labour cost was mechanisation. In 1872 there was only one reaper per eight men employed in the wheat fields of Santa Fe. By 1895 this ratio was 1:3·5 persons employed. In the case of threshers the ratio changed from 1:172 persons employed in 1872 to 1:36 in 1895.[5]

The Argentine system of cereal production was much criticised by contemporary observers, such as Bialet-Massé, who reported to the national government on the condition of the Argentine working class at the turn of the century, and by scholars since on account of careless methods, poor quality of products, indifference to social amenities, and the exploitation of farm workers by farmers and of farmers by landlords and middlemen. Not everything is known about Argentine cereal growers. We know where they came from: some of the earlier colonists were from Switzerland, Germany and Britain, and some were Jews from central Europe. The majority came from northern Italy and many from northern Spain. But we know little about what happened to them; whether they constituted a stable population which remained in the wheat growing business and in Argentina; whether those who were the 'Italian wheat kings' moved on and up—or out of Argentine society; whether the harvest labourer of one season was the wheat farmer of the next. We do know, however, that as a result of the development of the wheat economy literacy increased in a province like Santa Fe from less than 17 per cent at the time of the census of 1869 to better than 52 per cent in 1895.[6] We know, too, that the Argentine cereal farmer never had much trouble about mortgage indebtedness because the rental system of crops shares spread the risk of drought, pests and price fluctuations between landlord and tenant. The farmer moved his crop quickly with little social or individual investment in storage. He did not grade or clean his product, nor did anyone else until the product reached Liverpool (where a high percentage of it went). But it was competitive with other suppliers of the world market. Argentine cereals established themselves in the world market at times of falling prices for cereals and adverse terms of trade for the Argentine economy as a whole. They were able to do so for recognisable economic reasons: low cost of production and marketing. The factors in these low costs were several: virgin soil of seemingly inexhaustible fertility which compensated for droughts and pests, the big factors in risk; a climate that made few demands for capital investment in housing people and storing products; a location close to the points of embarkation for overseas markets (Argentine cereals travelled at most 200 miles to ports of embarkation and much of it less than 100 miles); limitation of capital investment strictly to labour-saving machinery in phases of production where labour costs were high; selling for gold-backed currencies and paying in paper currency which allowed for small economies in wages and in capital indebtedness; large-scale production; simplicity in handling and marketing.

The development of an international market for Argentine cereals produced a change in the marketing mechanisms. Cereals sold for local consumption by millers, oil processors and stock feeders were handled by middlemen operating competitively in centres like Buenos Aires, Rosario, Santa Fe and Córdoba. The overseas trade was handled predominantly by big mercantile enterprises with a good knowledge of the European markets and the capital to charter vessels and to handle, grade and clean the grain. Firms like Bunge y Born and Dreyfus were well established in the trade by 1890. They worked through middlemen, the *acopiadores*, who purchased crops, advanced working capital to farmers, rented machinery to them and carried them in bad years. This system contained the possibility of debt slavery, but so long as production was expanding and land was readily available the answer of the farmer to a bad situation was to move or quit. The marketing of frozen and chilled meat overseas at first involved comparatively small changes in the slaughtering industry. The *saladeros* producing salted meat, the tallow renderers and the producers of meat extract required only a comparatively small additional investment to commence freezing mutton. The carcase of a sheep could be manhandled, and did not require machinery to move it. In 1882 Eugenio Terrason converted his *saladero* to a *frigorífico*, and despatched the first frozen mutton to the British market in a British vessel fitted with Bell-Colman refrigerating apparatus, which had been developed with the advice of the professor of physics at Glasgow University, Sir William Thompson (later Lord Kelvin). Another Argentine firm, D. G. Sansinena y Cia, followed. These firms followed their traditional commercial practice of buying their raw material outright and selling their products outright through agents abroad. Unlike the Australian freezers, they did not work on account for sheep masters. Nor did they abandon their local market. They conducted their operations in Buenos Aires, which was not only a port of embarkation for exports but an important local market for their produce.

Simultaneously in 1882 an Anglo-Argentina businessman connected with banking and railways, George W. Drabble, founded the River Plate Fresh Meat Company Ltd, with a capital of £100,000 put up by the directors. This firm, starting from scratch with the object of developing a new trade, did not have an easy time of it. The same can be said of an attempt on

c

the part of a group of *estancieros* to found a producers' co-operative, La Congeladora Argentina. The problem seems to have been premature specialisation involving a total dependence on overseas markets and the installation of expensive, complicated equipment by the River Plate company at Campaña on the Paraná and at Colonia in Uruguay where skilled labour was scarce or non-existent. There was, too, the technical problem involved in freezing and chilling beef rather than sheep. The River Plate company made no profits and required fresh investments of capital and much reorganisation. At the same time it applied to the government for tax exemptions which were given in 1884 and finally for a system of guaranteeing profits generally on investments in *frigoríficos*.

If the success of the Argentine firms in the export of frozen meat illustrated the importance of expanding on the basis of a sustained cash flow generated in established local markets, a variation of the same strategy was likewise illustrated by the firm of James Nelson and Sons, a firm already well established in the live cattle trade. In 1886 this firm sent Hugh Nelson to Argentina to extend the operations of the firm into killing and freezing while maintaining its established line of business. The Nelsons built a *frigorífico* at Zarate on the river above Buenos Aires, and prospered.

The early history of the Argentine trade overseas in meat illustrates the importance of marketing in successful development. The French were technological pioneers in this activity, but commercially they achieved nothing because France was not a free, international market for meat, and the French lacked a strong position in the best free and open market: Britain. Being both British and Argentine, as the River Plate Fresh Meat Co Ltd was, provided no guarantee of success when it lacked market experience and outlets in both Britain and Argentina. When finally the Argentine meat trade established a fairly fixed character early in the twentieth century, it was seen that big firms, both British and American, with strong market positions came to dominate the field.

TABLE 2

Some indicators of economic growth and change, 1870–1890[7]

Year	Exports by value (in millions of hard pesos)								Exports (metric tons)		Imports (metric tons)	
	Wool	Hides	Dried and salted meat	Live animals	Tallow and guano	Hogs	Frozen mutton	Meat extract	Wheat	Flour	Wheat	Flour
1870	6·8	10·3	1·2	—	6·6	—	—	—	—	—	3,903	5,726
1871	7·4	8·9	1·1	—	4·5	—	—	—	9	17	1,524	5,681
1872	16·3	15·2	2·1	—	7·4	—	—	—	17	206	1,425	2,141
1873	19·6	14·3	1·4	—	5·5	—	—	—	5	122	1,055	1,017
1874	17·9	16·5	1·0	—	2·1	—	—	—	358	24	2,550	7,451
1875	19·9	17·4	1·4	—	4·7	—	—	—	—	13	4,887	16,923
1876	19·6	13·2	2·0	3·3	5·6	0·89	—	—	21	353	335	3,130
1877	18·1	12·1	2·7	3·9	4·1	0·68	—	—	200	218	600	128
1878	14·7	11·1	2·3	2·4	3·2	0·66	—	—	2,547	2,919	10	6
1879	21·6	13·1	2·8	2·1	2·0	0·76	—	—	25,669	1,603	6	4
1880	26·5	17·9	2·9	1·4	1·7	0·74	—	—	1,168	1,428	18,581	1,265
1881	30·4	14·5	2·5	2·1	1·4	0·75	—	—	157	1,287	11,478	2
1882	29·0	13·5	3·7	1·5	2·7	0·88	—	—	1,705	549	200	—
1883	29·6	15·2	2·8	2·1	2·5	0·69	0·011	—	60,755	4,844	230	—
1884	32·0	15·8	2·4	2·1	2·2	0·86	0·033	—	108,449	3,734	0·1	117
1885	35·9	20·8	4·2	2·5	3·5	1·0	0·075	—	78,493	7,447	17	3
1886	31·7	17·8	3·7	2·4	1·7	0·77	0·36	0·14	37,864	5,262	4	14
1887	32·7	21·1	2·3	1·6	2·1	0·98	0·96	0·085	237,866	5,501	42	5
1888	44·8	22·6	3·4	2·0	3·3	1·2	1·4	0·2	178,929	6,392	88	12
1889	56·7	20·1	6·1	3·6	0·54	1·1	1·3	0·181	22,806	3,361	3,051	61
1890	35·5	20·0	3·9	4·5	2·0	0·93	1·6	0·375	327,894	12,018	1,306	22

The growth of the economy during the years between 1870 and 1890 can be indicated by a variety of measures. International trade figures are, of course, no necessary or complete indication of economic growth, but given the character of the development of Argentina in these years they are suggestive.

During the two decades the population of Argentina almost doubled from approximately 1,800,000 to approximately 3,600,000. More than 60 per cent of this growth in population was accounted for by net immigration. The composition of the net immigration varied from year to year, but it was from 53 per cent to 71 per cent Italian and from 10 to 20 per cent Spanish between 1870 and 1890. French immigration to Argentina was significant, from 8 to 15 per cent of the total until 1890, but fell off sharply thereafter. British immigrants accounted for only 2 per cent to slightly less than 4 per cent during the years 1870–90 and fell off sharply after 1890. The immigrants taken altogether were overwhelmingly artisans and agricultural workers.

The role of the state in inducing immigration was at first a limited one. From the late 1860s immigration agents advertised the advantages of migration to Argentina, but inducements to emigrate to Argentina consisted more of the government's foregoing revenue and other requirements than of positive subventions. Colonising companies, colonists and the tools of colonists were exempt from taxation. The colonists themselves were exempt from military service. The immigration law of 1876 enabled the government to pay a small subsidy in the shape of five days' free board and lodging for immigrants on disembarkation with the right to a further extension at a low rate. Most immigrants financed themselves, or were assisted by colonising companies or groups in their country of origin interested in planting colonies in Argentina, such as the Welsh in the Chubut and the Jews in Entre Rios, Santa Fe and interior provinces. The lack of harvest hands in the late 1880s induced the national government to provide free passage for 12,000 immigrants in 1888, for 100,000 in 1889 and for 20,000 in 1890. An important agency in inducing immigration was the shipping companies who had a commercial interest in filling their ships:

live cattle one way and live workers the other. When all the abuses of immigration have been recounted and all the tales of horror told, it remains a fact that large numbers of people flowed across the Atlantic to Argentina without political or physical compulsion in response to economic inducements. The deceit of profiteering agents and the desire to flee military service may have influenced some, but those who migrated did not all become prisoners of circumstance in Argentina. There was an emigration from Argentina as well as immigration into the Republic. In 1891 after the Baring crisis had broken on the economy 20,000 more people left Argentina than entered, and it was an exceptional year when less than 40 per cent of the number who entered did not leave. 1882 was such an exceptional year when the emigrants amounted to only 8 per cent of the immigrants.

The growth of production in the countryside had consequences for the cities and created there the necessity for large investments of capital. In 1870 Buenos Aires was a city of less than 200,000 inhabitants spread out along the *baranca* of the Río de la Plata so that the countryside was never far away. Even so the congregation of so many people living in close proximity to one another had begun to present problems of health. In 1868 there had been a frightening outbreak of cholera. Water drawn from the shallow foreshore of the river into which sewage emptied and in which people washed, delivered moreover from wooden water carts, was no longer a possible way of supplying an essential of existence. The government of the province of Buenos Aires borrowed money in Britain and established a waterworks and sewage system, but energetic action and large investments in plant hardly kept pace with the growth of the city. Cholera and yellow fever were recurring terrors through the 1870s. In 1880, Buenos Aires became a federal territory, the seat of the national government and thus under the control of the power with the greatest taxing capacity. Thereafter, the redevelopment of the city commenced, being financed by large borrowing. It was in fact the financing of water works in Buenos Aires which precipitated the Baring crisis of 1890–1.

The great increase in overseas trade made urgent the building of harbour works. Buenos Aires is not a good natural harbour. The river Plate has extensive shallows before the shore is reached, and ships had always been obliged to anchor far out in the river and unload into tenders or high wheeled carts. The winds in the estuary were perilous both to ships and those ashore; to the first because the winds often blew with gale force inland, and to the second because they caused flooding. The need for harbour works, the deepening and clearing of channels from deep water and the provision of warehousing and handling facilities became increasingly urgent both at Buenos Aires and at Rosario. Again, heavy investments of capital in construction work and machinery were required. These were made on an increasing scale, particularly after 1880.

Surface transport in the cities and gas lighting were left to private enterprise, largely foreign and mainly British. Franchises were freely granted by the public authorities as a result of which there was much competition, duplication of services, and bankruptcies and mergers. Public transport was an activity where the foreign entrepreneurs and investors made the most direct and continuous contact with the local consumers, and this was a source of contention, irritation, corruption and ill-will out of all proportion to the size of the investment and the profits earned. If there had been any overall strategy of foreign investors they might have left urban transport to local private or municipal enterprise.

No account of the economic development of the years 1870–90 can be complete or even comprehensible which does not call attention to the political action of the Argentine public authorities in creating the conditions for development and the dynamic of self-interest which produced the effects which the leaders intended. Of these political acts undoubtedly the most important was the destruction of the Indians of the pampas by the military campaigns led by General Julio Roca: the *salidas de Roca*. For at least two centuries the Indians had disputed the control of the resources of the pampas with the Spaniards and Argentines. Until the mid-1880s they drove off cattle from the ranches in the provinces of the Litoral for their own use and for the purpose of trade through the passes of the Andes to Chile.

The Indian menace was one of the important reasons given by Consul-General MacDonnell in 1872 why the British government should discourage immigration of British subjects to Argentina. So long as there was no very marked difference between the way the *estancieros* and *saladeros* exploited the resources of the pampas and the way the Indians did, there was a possibility of uneasy peace and a rough sharing of the bounty of nature. Two centuries of relations between the Indians and the Hispano-Argentines suggest that this possibility had often been a reality. However, once the Argentines began to discover the more intensive use of the pampas, and its profitability, the possibilities of the past began to change and of peace to diminish. The disparity in power began to grow so that the Argentines had the power of decision increasingly in their hands. Under the leadership of President Avellaneda and General Roca they used it with merciless thoroughness. The Indians were massacred, and those who escaped death found refuge as wanderers in the remote parts of Patagonia and in Chile or were absorbed into the labour market as servants and peons.

The destruction of the Indians was followed by a plentiful distribution of land to officers, soldiers and friends of the government. President Avellaneda's efforts to inaugurate a system of open, egalitarian distribution were ineffective. The class of landed proprietors was both enlarged and enriched with resources. But the new lands cleared of Indians in the south and south-west of the provinces of Buenos Aires, Córdoba and San Luis and in the unorganised territories further south were valueless or nearly so unless they could be rendered productive and the products marketed. The ranchers and sheep masters had long been the dynamic element in the development of the economy. Their new possessions and the increase in their numbers and opportunities made them more so. The demand for more capital investment and more market opportunities intensified. Concretely this meant railways, and ancillary to them handling, processing and warehousing equipment and ocean-going shipping. A parallelism of interest between land-owners, the agencies of government, the investing classes locally and internationally, and the professions came into being which imparted a powerful forward momentum to Argentine society. The scepticism, hostility and condemnation with which today this phase of Argentine history is regarded was almost wholly absent when it was taking place, and a popular optimism deriving from existing experience all but silenced those who for one reason or another questioned the value of what was happening and how. The generation of the 1880s were pleased with themselves, and Argentine society remained on balance pleased for another forty years.

Notes to this chapter are on p 193

5
The Baring crisis and after,
1890-1899

The rapid economic development of the years 1870–90 was supported by heavy flows of capital and labour from Europe. The resources of the Argentine Republic had attracted these factors of production, and land, labour and capital then became fruitful. In the year 1888 new issues on behalf of Argentine governments and enterprises in Argentina on the London exchange had a value of 79 million gold pesos, and in 1889 of 69 million gold pesos, compared with issues valued at only 16 million gold pesos in 1884.[1] Net immigration into Argentina from Europe in 1884 was 63,300; in 1888 it was 138,700 and in 1889 200,000.[2] Then there was suddenly a sharp fall in investment and immigration. Between 1890 and the end of the century, the process of investment and immigration stagnated. New issues for Argentina in London fell to 30 million gold pesos in 1890; to 11 million in 1891; to 3 million in 1892; to 1 million in 1895, and rose thereafter to a modest 13 million in 1900. In 1891 there was net emigration from Argentina of 29,800 people. In 1892 net immigration recommenced at 29,400 people, and until 1904 fluctuated at a figure less than 50,000 annually except in 1896 when 89,200 people appear to have opted to remain in Argentina.

The stagnation in investment and immigration of the 1890s compared with what had gone before and what was to follow from the turn of the century to the years 1913–14 was not, however, an indication of a stagnant economy. Far from it.

Wheat acreage increased from three million acres in 1890 to eight million in 1900. Production of wheat rose from 850,000 metric tons in 1890 to 2,750,000 metric tons in 1900. Exports of wheat rose from 327,894 metric tons in 1890 to 1,929,676 metric tons in 1900 and exports of flour from 12,018 metric tons in 1890 to 51,203 metric tons in 1900.[3] The average annual export of meat in various forms during the years 1880–9 was 34,016 tons; the average during the 1890s was 84,433 tons.[4] The absence of statistics before 1895 makes it difficult to indicate industrial growth. The first census which produced information on this subject showed that in 1895 industrial capital was worth 500 million paper pesos and used engines producing 60,000 horsepower.[5]

In terms of production and trade the decade of the 1890s was, thus, far from static, but it was none the less a decade of reorganisation and uncertainty, which began with the Baring crisis of 1890–1 and concluded with the Conversion Law of 1899 and the establishment of the Caja de Conversión. This put Argentina effectively on the gold standard after nearly ninety years of failed attempts to achieve stability of the currency.

The arrest in the flow of capital and labour to Argentina first began to manifest itself in investment. In 1889 there was a falling-off from the unexpectedly high level of 1888. Throughout 1889 signs began to emerge calculated to frighten the investing classes in Europe and to deflate the Argentine balloon blown up with optimism, hope and greed. There was, to begin with, the prospect early in 1889 of a poor crop. The gold premium began to rise. In 1887 it had averaged only 35; in 1888 it had been 48; in 1889 it averaged 94, and by the end of the year it required more than two paper pesos to pay a debt of one peso written in terms of gold or gold-backed currency. Then the Argentine government proposed to pay the interest and sinking fund charges on the Hard Dollar Loan of 1872 in soft dollars, ie in paper pesos. By September 1889, those in the know, the bankers and underwriters, were well aware of the fact that the Argentine government could no longer pay its obligations in full, and that the public revenues and the economy from which they were derived were unequal to the full burden of interest, sinking fund charges, debenture charges and guaranteed profits which had been accumulated during two decades of increasingly rapid development. The bankers and underwriters in London and Paris tried desperately to put on a brave face. They borrowed to the hilt in order to honour the bills coming in from contractors. They proposed a halt in investment in Argentina for ten years. This was an otiose proposal inasmuch as the halt was already in being, created by the growing scepticism of the investing public. The net effect of the struggles of the bankers and underwriters in Europe was not to keep the investment process rolling but only to sustain the stock market value of existing Argentine securities. These lost less than 10 per cent of their market value during the last months of 1889 and the first half of 1890. It was only after the bankers, under the leadership of the Bank of England and the British Chancellor of the Exchequer, were obliged to come to the rescue of Baring Brothers that the real collapse on the Stock Exchange came about. This cut the market values of Argentine securities roughly in half.

While the flow of investment funds was thus freezing to a halt in Europe, events in Argentina were becoming increasingly tense both economically and politically. The effect of the gold premium on real wages was severe in 1889 and 1890. The premium of 91 in 1889 rose to 151 in 1890, and some idea of its catastrophic character can be gained by looking at the peak figure in 1894: 257. The paper price of practically everything bought with paper wages mounted terribly. A calculation made by Williams indicates that rural wages increased only by 79 per cent between 1883 and 1891–2, whereas the gold premium increased by 232 per cent.[6] The effect of this on domestic prices of consumer goods has not yet been measured, but the evidence of observers is unmistakably that this imbalance between increases in the gold premium and increases in wages meant declining real wages. As early as 1887 the *South American Journal*, an English-language weekly devoted to economic affairs, noted that there was serious discontent among wage-workers and that mounting prices were eating up nominally high wages so that skilled workers were no longer able to save and buy property. Strikes grew, and trade unions began to form. Some employers

attempted to ease the position of their employees, as the Ferrocarril Sud did, by paying its permanent staff 50 per cent in
gold. Only an injection of subsidy into the immigration process
by the Argentine government kept up the flow of immigrants in
1889. In 1890 the flow ceased, and people fled, so bad had the
conditions of the wage-working class become.

The professional and property-owning classes were equally
disturbed, but in a different way. The government of President
Juárez Celman had quite clear ideas about what needed to be
done. The President proposed to Congress in March 1890 that
public expenditure be cut; that the public revenues be increased by the imposition of gold customs duties; that the policy
of guaranteeing railway profits be terminated; and that an in-
quiry be instituted into the operation of joint stock companies.
Central to the presidential programme was a recognition of the
effect of a paper currency and loose credit policies by the banks
upon the public revenues. The estimated service charges on
Argentine borrowings had risen from 23 million gold pesos in
1885 to 60 millions in 1890,[7] but actual gold receipts for the year
1891 were only a miserable 497,121 gold pesos.[8] The rest of the
Argentine revenues were paid in paper pesos. By 1891 about $2\frac{1}{2}$
paper pesos were required to do the work of 1 gold peso. And
the claims of the creditors of Argentina were payable in
gold.

At the best of times the Argentine revenue system was shaky,
particularly the provincial revenues. The province of Buenos
Aires, for example, collected on average only 6 million paper
pesos a year in 1889–91 and spent 17 millions a year on ordinary
account.[9] The national government was in better shape than
this, but its revenues were heavily derived from customs and
excise duties which in turn depended on the level of economic
activity. Furthermore, many imports such as much railway
equipment had been exempt from all taxation as a result of
agreements about franchises, and certain exports such as
cereals and frozen meat had been exempted from export duties
as part of a development plan. A policy of imposing gold duties
was in effect a policy of increasing taxation. The politicians in
the Congress were much more hesitant about such a policy than

the railway companies which imposed gold freight tariffs in order to keep solvent.

President Juárez Celman may have known what to do but he lacked the political will and support to impose a policy. Early in April 1890 there were great popular demonstrations against the government organised by a newly founded dissident political group, the Unión Cívica. In response to this Juárez appointed a new Minister of Finance, Dr Jose E. Uriburu. Uriburu's policy was to increase customs duties by 15 per cent and collect half of them in gold. He published a report of the Inspector of Banks concerning breaches of the law governing the Guaranteed Banks, and he demanded that the President of the Banco Nacional be removed from office. Faced with this demand, President Juárez Celman refused, and Uriburu resigned. The gold premium jumped from 118 to 165 in one day.

Uriburu had in mind a funding loan in Europe designed to meet the obligations to foreign creditors, an increase in taxation and the purge of the Argentine banks, which was one of the conditions required by the bankers in Europe. Uriburu had already tried to find bankers softer than those who operated in London, but he had been disappointed. The German bankers, for example, told him that they had the fullest confidence in the prospects of Argentina, if the Argentine government would impose gold customs duties and a land tax, stop the marketing of land mortgage bonds and improve the administration of land sales by provincial governments. This was much more bitter medicine than the British bankers prescribed, but milder than that of the Americans, a fact discovered when the next President of Argentina made a tentative exploration of what might be got from New York and Washington.

Students of Argentine economic experience thinking about the problems which faced the Argentines in the 1890s today ask the question: should Juárez Celman have let Argentina go bankrupt? After all, investment and immigration had transformed the economy and laid the foundations for the expansion of production. Bankruptcy could not remove the railways or destroy the grain farms or the packing plants or the markets overseas. Why not go bankrupt, and then strike out on their own relying on their own capacity to accumulate capital and to undertake a more substantial part of their own investment than hitherto?

Whether this would have been possible, and, if possible, the right course for Argentina remains an open question. What happened was a revolution which forced Juárez Celman to resign the presidency. This revolt was the work of the Unión Cívica in the last week of July 1890. Heavy fighting in the city of Buenos Aires produced the fall of the government, but not the fall of the interests concerned in development along the lines already established. The Vice-President, Carlos Pellegrini, became President, and he superintended a change of course, if not a change of the objectives of economic policy.

Pellegrini's Minister of Finance, Vicente Lopez, commenced a harsh house-cleaning operation. He told the nation that inflation had reduced real public revenues by 50 per cent. He proposed to increase taxes, to stop further issues of paper currency, to require a close scrutiny of banking practices and the conduct of the municipal authorities in the city of Buenos Aires and to end the system of guaranteeing profits on railways. A 60 per cent increase in import duties on tobacco, imported foods, imported clothing and works of art was decreed, and the collection of all duties in gold. Import duties on productive equipment were simultaneously reduced or abolished.

While these measures were being developed and applied during the last quarter of 1890, Baring Brothers in the City of London were going broke. The affairs of Barings were complicated, but the explanation of their situation is simple. In 1888 they underwrote the Buenos Aires Water Supply and Drainage Loan of 25 million dollars. In return for 25 million in gold bonds Barings undertook to pay 21 million gold in three instalments and in the form either of cash or of bills drawn on them by engineering and supply contractors. The events of 1889 and 1890, the rising gold premium, news of strikes, bankruptcies, distress among the immigrants, and failures to pay interest on bonds in hard currency combined to kill the market for Buenos Aires Water Supply and Drainage Bonds. Barings could not sell them at any price, and the bills of the contractors and suppliers began pouring in. Barings borrowed and borrowed in spite of a high bank rate. Then lenders began to call a halt. Barings were staring in the face of bankruptcy.

And maybe the City of London, too. The Chancellor of the Exchequer and the Governor of the Bank of England were quick to see that the failure of Barings would bring on a smoking financial collapse affecting the whole economy and the position of Britain as an international financial centre. They quickly and quietly joined forces to bail out Barings and save the reputation of the British banking and underwriting system. This was the first instance of an essential modification of the *laissez faire* system; that if an enterprise is big enough it cannot be allowed to fail no matter how badly run. The first lame duck had been hatched.

Briefly stated, the Chancellor of the Exchequer undertook on behalf of the British government and taxpayers to underwrite the Bank of England, which in turn undertook to underwrite the leading banks in the City of London in subscribing to a loan fund which was to be used to pay the creditors of Barings cent per cent. The lenders expected to recover their money from the liquidation of Barings. If they did not, they would not lose because the British taxpayers would have to pay.

Once it was decided who was going to pick up the bill, a committee was formed under the chairmanship of the Roths-childs to deal with the whole question of the Argentine default. The policy of Pellegrini and Vicente Lopez was to pay if they could: the policy of the Rothschild committee was to get their pound of flesh if they could. The Rothschild committee was representative of various financial interests, British, French and German, and these were divided in their approach to the problem of getting as much as they could. The British, and parti-cularly the Rothschilds, took what may be called a liberal view, ie they would lend Argentina more money to pay the interest and sinking fund charges on its existing debts. They based this view on confidence in the potential for growth of the Argentine economy. If Argentina could not pay its existing debts now it could pay a larger debt later. The French and German views tended to be much stricter. Argentine ought to pay out of current resources and ought to tax heavily enough to do so. Observers like *The Economist* declared for strict policies on the grounds of commercial morality and for the very good reason that the investing public would never buy Argentine securities so long as it was plain that the Argentine government was paying interest and sinking fund charges out of fresh borrowings and was thus pyramiding debts to put off the day of settlement. *The Economist* saw the whole operation as a device for keeping up the price of Argentine securities while the liquidators of Barings were unloading their holdings on a wider public destined to pay now and suffer later.

1891 was a bad year for all concerned. The net value in gold pesos of Argentine exports rose only slightly to 103 million in 1891 compared with 101 million in 1890 and 123 million in 1889. This was, however, achieved in spite of a falling-off of prices.[10] Imports were down from 165 million gold pesos in 1889 to 67 million in 1891. Foreign borrowing was down from 248 million gold pesos in 1888 and 45 million in 1890 to 8 million in 1891, most of it on account of the Rothschild funding loan.[11] The gold premium averaged an all-time high of 287 per cent in 1891.

In 1892 Pellegrini was occupied with political problems. He superintended the election of his successor in the presidency, Dr Luis Saenz Peña. Saenz chose as his Minister of Finance Dr J. J. Romero, a man who in the past had attempted unsuccessfully to establish a hard currency in Argentina. Romero rejected the idea of paying interest and sinking fund charges out of borrowings. In November 1893, he declared in a letter to the press that Argentina was not paying its way. He removed the Argentine financial representative in London. Then he set about negotiating an agreement with the Rothschild Committee based on paying what Argentina could pay. The *Arreglo Romero* signed in July 1893 committed the bankers to suspending all sinking fund charges until 1901 and cutting the rate of interest on outstanding debts by approximately 30 per cent. In return the Argentine government gave up all claims in connection with the underwriting of the Buenos Aires Water Supply and Drainage Loan, agreed to take over the debts of the

Argentine provinces and to pay them at something approximating to 80 cents in the dollar, and agreed to pay a lump sum to discharge obligations under guarantee clauses in railway contracts and to end the system of guarantees.

Underlying the settlement of the financial problem were political and economic developments. A business settlement of the kind achieved by Romero was possible because the European governments, and particularly the British government which had been approached by a group of bankers, refused absolutely to interfere in Argentine affairs or to force the Argentine government to accept financial advisers whose business it would be to run Argentina in the interest of and in accordance with the policies of European financial leaders. Likewise the Argentine government was firm in its determination to admit no intervention in its affairs, and was not prepared to see any modification of international practice designed to countenance the interference of foreign powers in its negotiations with bankers and mercantile interests.[12]

The economic developments of the 1890s provided the means of preserving and eventually expanding the integration of the Argentine economy in the world economy and the linking of Argentina with the growth, principally, of the western European economy. The massive investment of the late 1880s began to pay off in the 1890s. In spite of the abundant fraud and misapplication of funds, the money borrowed by Argentina and the purchasing power made available to railway entrepreneurs, harbour companies and municipal authorities was in the main used to finance real production: to haul grain, to slaughter cattle, to freeze meat, to load cargoes and to preserve and improve the health of the community.

Contemporary discussion of the Baring crisis laid great emphasis on fraud, speculation and corrupt influences upon the public authorities as explanatory factors in the financial collapse. Subsequent study of the crisis reveals that an important element in the failure of the Argentine economy in the early 1890s to generate enough saleable commodities to meet the expectations of the investors was the method of financing itself. The capitalists who invested in Argentine enterprises in the

1880s conformed very little to the image of the capitalist presented by the economic theoreticians of the age. They were not bold risk-takers whose rewards for good judgement in the presence of uncertainty were handsome profits and whose punishment was loss and possible bankruptcy. The capitalists wanted certainty *and* income from their investments. Nearly half of the Argentine obligations to investors in 1890 was fixed-interest bonds of public authorities (28 million gold pesos out of 60 million of debt service charges). Of the remaining charges of 32 million gold pesos in the private sector much was on account of guaranteed profits, but more was due to holders of debentures. Less than 30 per cent of railway capital, for example, was share capital.[13] This meant that enterprises like railways, port-works, gasworks and waterworks, which took anything from six months to 4–5 years to build and bring into production, were loaded with capital charges from the moment the money to finance them was raised. Rothschilds were right when they based their policy of a funding loan on the expectation that Argentina would eventually be able to pay, but this understanding did not prevent crisis any more than their solution could restore a healthy capital flow into further development.

Given the fact that investment had been made in equipping productive enterprises, the capacity of these enterprises to meet all claims upon them by investors depended on two variable factors: the cost of labour and the price of the end-products in the markets available to them. The data do not exist or have not yet been assembled to give a global account of wages in the form of statistical tables in a time series, but the observations of journalists and others indicate that from 1887 onward the effect of inflation on the real income of wage-workers was seriously adverse. The real cost of labour to the purchasers—ranchers, share-cropping cereal growers, railway enterprises, packing plants, stevedoring firms and manufacturers—was falling, and continued to fall until 1895, when the gold premium began to fall.

Monetary and credit factors were not alone in having a depressing effect on labour costs. It is true that immigration became negative in 1891, and remained low compared with the 1880s until 1896, but this was not decisive in its effect on labour supply. The cessation of capital investment and the completion of the projection undertaken in the late 1880s threw men on to the labour market. Not everyone could or would return to Italy or Spain. The result was intensified competition for jobs in the agricultural sector and in urban processing and handling enterprises. Competition had a full effect on wages because there was little in the way of collective bargaining or agencies of relief for the workless. Enterprises such as railways, vulnerable to unorganised strikes of desperation, were able to ward off serious trouble because they themselves were masters of a necessity of other producers, and could, and did, move their rates upward with the gold premium and their wages similarly but not always in the same degree. In the case of farmers, ranchers and small business enterprises desperation worked the other way and to their advantage.

Except in the year 1892 the price variable was adverse for the main Argentine producers until 1897, and in the pastoral sector remained so until 1899.[14] Low wage costs and low ocean freights, however, made it possible for Argentine producers to expand. The receipts from wool sales abroad, for example, during the years 1890-9 were 411 million gold pesos compared with 359 million gold pesos during the years 1880-9. The totals of the years 1890-9 were achieved in the face of a pastoral export price index which ran (1900 = 100):

1890—102	1895— 62
1891— 88	1896— 70
1892—102	1897— 74
1893— 71	1898— 75
1894— 63	1899—108

The receipts from frozen mutton were enormously expanded during the decade. The receipts from the export of live cattle for the years 1890-4 inclusive were 8½ million gold pesos more than for the whole decade of the 1880s and for the years 1895-9 inclusive were 13 million gold pesos greater.[15]

During the 1880s the balance of trade between Argentina and

the rest of the world on commodity account had been unfavourable. During the years 1886–90 inclusive, Argentina
imported goods valued at 647 million gold pesos and exported
goods valued at only 378 million. In 1891 the balance of trade
became favourable to Argentina and remained so except in 1893
when imports exceeded exports by two million gold pesos.
During the years 1891–1900 inclusive the overall favourable
balance of Argentina on commodity account was 235 million
gold pesos, and 137 million of this was earned in the years
1898–1900 inclusive.[16]

These changes were due, on the one hand, to the drastic re-
duction in capital investment and the purchases made of capital
equipment and, on the other, by the rise in the volume of
exports. After 1897 another factor began to operate: the improvement in prices and the terms of trade. Ford's study of the
Argentine prices indicates that, apart from the exceptional year
1892, when the terms were 126 (1900 = 100), the terms of
trade ran:

1893—	94	1897—109	
1894—	88	1898—106	
1895—	86	1899—110	
1896—	93		

The combined effect of the increase in the volume of exports
and the improvement of prices relative to outgoings in payment
for imports was a decline in the gold premium. Gold and gold-
backed currencies were increasingly obtainable by Argentine
citizens and the Argentine public authorities. As a result fewer
and fewer paper pesos were required to purchase gold. Put the
other way round, the person who paid for produce in gold could
buy fewer and fewer paper pesos. So far as it concerned
ranchers and cereal producers, the shoe was now on the other
foot. Wages paid in paper, interest paid in paper and other
costs paid in paper began to absorb more and more of their
receipts. A shift of income unfavourable to them began to
develop as the gold premium fell. In August 1898, for example,
the gold premium was 176; by December it had fallen to 112.
The impact of a decline of this description upon producers pay-

ing wages and other costs in paper was severe. They cried out, and they were heard by the government.

In the face of violent opposition from economic theorists and from creditor interests holding assets written in gold-backed currencies the Finance Minister, Dr J. M. Rosa, forced through Congress the Conversion Law of 1899. The object of the law was to arrest the decline of the gold premium. The effect was to stabilise the currency and in effect to put Argentina on the gold standard, where it remained for thirty-five years. The Conversion Law fixed the exchange rate of the paper peso at 227·24 paper pesos for 100 gold pesos as defined by the Law of 1875. The law provided for a Caja de Conversión, or Conversion Office, which could buy and sell gold at the fixed rate of conversion. Any further emissions of currency would have to be covered cent per cent with gold. Thus, the Argentine paper currency was tied to gold so that at the date of the promulgation of the law there was one gold peso available for every 2·27 paper pesos and any further paper pesos put in circulation would have to be backed by one gold peso for each paper peso issued.[17] The circulating medium henceforth fluctuated in volume within narrow limits. From 1900 onward it was in the neighbourhood of 100–110 pesos per head and it was 111 in 1929, although during the last years of World War I it rose, and reached a maximum of 156 pesos per head in 1920.[18]

Although there was some buying and selling of gold on the exchanges and by private transactions for a few years following the Conversion Law, the market in gold and the gold premium soon ceased to exist as a factor in the economic and commercial life of the country. Thus, the economy was rendered more independent of political influences, and economic decision-making conformed more to the market pattern of classical *laissez faire* theory.

This was one consequence of the Baring crisis and its resolution. In another respect the *laissez faire* system was more completely established. During the year after the writing of the constitution of 1853 the liberal intentions of its creators had been much modified in practice by the heavy involvement of the state in the initiation and guarantee of investment in railways, port works and meat packing and in the movement of labour to the republic. After 1890 the role of the state began to diminish, partly as a result of bankruptcy or threatened bankruptcy and partly as a conscious policy of politicians like Juárez Celman, Roca and Pellegrini who believed that the state was a bad organiser and master of productive enterprises. To stave off ruin the province of Buenos Aires sold the Ferrocarril Oeste to a British syndicate. In order to build up the gold reserves of the Caja de Conversión, the government sold the Ferrocarril Andino to private investors. The trend towards private ownership of major productive equipment was thus intensified, and the public authorities concerned themselves henceforward more with the provision of services such as education, and the improvement and expansion of public amenities and institutions such as the armed forces.

Notes to this chapter are on pp 193–4

6

The golden age,
1899-1929

There is justification for considering the years 1899–1929 as a
unified phase of Argentine economic history. The phase opened
with the Conversion Law which established the free convertibility of peso into gold and it ended with the suspension of that
free convertibility on 16 December 1929. Although the gold
standard was one of the constants of this phase (interrupted in
its working by the period of World War I and its aftermath)
there were other features of the Argentine economy which enable one to describe these three decades as golden in more than
a monetary sense. They were decades of growth in population,
in the real income of that population, in total production, and
in capital stock.

TABLE 3

Economic growth of Argentina, 1900–1929[1]

Population (5-year averages, 000s of people)		Gross product (in millions of pesos at 1950 prices)	Capital stock (at current prices in millions of dollars)		Real wages in Buenos Aires index number	
1900–4	4·797	10·756	1900	3·500		
1905–9	5·710	15·890	1909	5·300		
1910–14	7·271	19·896	1913	6·530	1914	100
1915–19	8·372	19·131			1915–19	78
1920–4	9·416	25·491	1923	8·310	1920–4	113
1925–9	10·970	33·184	1927	10·200	1925–9	144

The unity of this phase was based on the persistence and

intensification of already established lines of production: agriculture, ranching and the processing and export of food products. In the years 1900–4 agriculture and ranching accounted for 38 per cent of the gross domestic product, in 1910–14 for 32·4 per cent and in 1925 for 30·8 per cent. This diminution in overall importance was only partially matched by the increase in mining, manufacturing and construction which increased from 12·9 per cent in 1900–4 and rose to 16·5 per cent in 1910–14, remaining stable at this proportion until 1929. The percentages of commerce, transport and finance all increased. These increases, like the increase in manufacturing, were associated with the agricultural and pastoral industry, particularly on the export side. This is demonstrated by an examination of the allocation of labour supplies which shows 39·2 per cent in agriculture and livestock in 1900–4 and 35·9 per cent in 1925–9; 19·8 per cent in industry in 1900–4 and 20·8 per cent in 1925–9.[2]

International trade continued to have a high and constant level of importance during these years. The proportion of the gross domestic product imported hovered around one quarter: 23·1 per cent during the years 1900–4, 26·2 per cent during 1910–14, and 22·6 per cent during 1925–9. Exports more than matched imports and were the means of paying for imports plus interest, sinking fund charges and profits on foreign investments in Argentina. In 1928–9 Argentina ranked eleventh among the major trading nations of the world with per capita exports of US $90 per annum compared with $105 for Australia, $125 for Canada, $72 for the United Kingdom, and $38.50 for the USA.

A fairly simple explanation of this character of the Argentine economy during the first three decades of the twentieth century springs readily to mind. The Argentines did what it was in their economic interest to do. Except during the years 1920–4 the terms on which Argentina traded with the rest of the world were exceptionally favourable: more favourable than they were in the nineteenth century and more favourable than they were ever to be again (except in the two years 1947 and 1948). Calculated on a base year 1950 as 100 the terms of trade for the years 1900–30 were:[3]

1900–4	110·6	1915–20	123·1
1905–9	129·7	1920–4	94·5
1910–14	129·8	1925–9	125·3

If investment flowed into agricultural and pastoral production and into the processing and marketing of natural products and not into activities like manufacturing it did so because this was profitable. But it was also beneficial on the whole to the community in spite of regional inequalities. Argentines had a better expectation of life than other peoples of South America and of many European peoples. The Argentine death rate in 1929 was 13·1 per thousand compared with 11·6 in the USA, 13·4 in Great Britain and 22·4 in Brazil. Argentines were more literate by 1929 than they had been in 1914. They possessed more motor vehicles per head of population than any European community, and more per head than they were to have again for another thirty years.[4] The Argentines in 1929 were a wealthy community. In 1940 Colin Clark ranked them with the USA, Canada, Australia, Switzerland, New Zealand and Great Britain as one of the countries with the highest standard of living in the world.[5]

This progress towards affluence was based upon an average growth in output of 4·6 per cent per annum for thirty years. A picture, however, of steady growth from 1899 to 1929 would be false. The rate of growth during the years 1899–1913 was almost double the rate from 1913 to 1929, and during the years 1917–21 was very low compared with the period as a whole. Díaz Alejandro has calculated a breakdown of growth as shown in Table 4.

TABLE 4

Rates of economic growth, 1900–1929[6]

	1900–4/ 1910–14	1910–14/ 1925–9
Population	4·3	2·8
Labour supply	4·4	2·2
Agriculture, livestock, fishing	3·0	2·6
Industry	5·8	1·7
Services	4·8	2·4

The pattern and direction of growth established between 1870 and 1890 and brought into a condition of balanced forward momentum during the 1890s was continued in circumstances of the international economy which were on the whole very favourable. Growth was achieved by bringing more land into production through the investment of more capital and the influx of more workers. The fundamental capital investment required to effect the use of more land continued to be the building of railways. Railway building and increased acreage devoted to cereal production, for example, were related as in Table 5.

TABLE 5

Railway building and cereal production, 1900–1930[7]

	Railways (ooos km)	Cereals sown (ooos hectares)
1900	16·6	4,614
1907	22·0	9,234
1914	33·5	12,560
1922	35·1	10,310
1929–30	38·9	16,757

The extension of railways, however, had begun to exhaust itself by 1914. There was a crisis of capital investment in 1913, and thereafter railway expansion slowed down. Indeed, during the years 1913–30 the railways grew less in length than they did between 1930 and their nationalisation in 1947, when there were 46,000 kilometres of railway in the Republic.

The years from the opening of the century to 1929 witnessed an expansion of the area devoted to the production of cereals to a near maximum. The area sown to wheat in 1928–9, 9,219,000 hectares, was never again exceeded. The area of the pampas given over to cattle reached its approximate maximum in the 1920s at approximately 45,000,000 hectares.[8] The economically active population in the rural sector reached 1,500,000 by the late 1920s, and, although it did reach a maximum of 2,000,000 in 1947, was already a sharply declining percentage of total population.[9]

The agricultural and pastoral undertakings which exploited approximately 65,000,000 hectares (or about 25 per cent of the area of the Republic) were private enterprises organised in a great variety of ways. In explaining the organisation of the agricultural and pastoral industry it is necessary to make a distinction between ownership of land and the units of production. These did not coincide. Some owners were producers. Many producers were not owners, and some producers were both owners and tenants of other owners. Some owners themselves organised production, and were working farmers or ranchers. Some owners depended on managers. Many owners were individuals; some were joint stock companies. A growing number were family companies organised to get round the inheritance laws which required the equal division of landed estates among heirs.

The units of ownership tended to be large, and the landlords of Argentina were famous for their vast estates and their fabulous wealth. Jaciento Oddone, who studied landownership in the 1930s, sought to measure the size and value of the large estates. In the province of Buenos Aires, for example, he found that in 1928 fifty families owned 4,663,575 hectares. The Luro family owned 411,938 hectares (approximately 1 million acres) which was valued for tax purposes at 111,826,700 gold pesos (approximately £5,000,000). This was both the largest and the most valuable holding. The Mulhalls, on the other hand, had to make do with a mere 63,457 hectares worth only 2,175,000 gold pesos. Size bore no necessary relationship to value. The Duranona family possessed only 32,281 hectares but these were valued for tax purposes at seven times the worth of the Mulhall estate, or roughly 14·15 times the value per hectare.[10] In the province of Entre Rios Oddone found that in 1930 34,994 proprietors owned 6,239,000 hectares, but 40 of these proprietors— some individuals, some joint stock companies—owned 1,338,749 hectares. In this province the descendants of the great caudillo, General Urquiza, who overthrew General Rosas and helped to found modern, liberal, capitalist Argentina, were the largest owners with the most valuable property: 151,829 hectares worth 18,669,975 gold pesos.[11] Even in the province of Santa

Fe, where colonists had been settled on small freeholds, large estates were common.

It would be painting a false picture to describe Argentine agriculture and ranching during the years 1900–30 in terms of large estates. In the first place it must be noticed that location and form of activity have a bearing on size of holding. A large estate close to the city of Buenos Aires or in the rich country around Pergamino was quite a different proposition from 10,000 hectares of land in the south of the province of La Pampa which might have enabled a single sheep farmer to get a living by hard work. Even today a rancher on marginal land, say in southern Corrientes, using modern equipment including an aeroplane for the purpose of travel and inspection can only break even on 10,000 hectares working fourteen hours a day. In the second place, it must also be noted that even in the province of Buenos Aires in 1914 70 per cent of the land holdings measured 5,000 hectares or less and nearly 40 per cent less than 1,000 hectares. Holdings under 100 hectares were not a viable proposition except as market gardens close to large centres of population. Historically the tendency has been for landholdings to diminish in size in response to market forces and changing techniques of production.

The essential point, however, in describing the rural economy as it existed in the years 1900–30 was the flexibility of the renting system. Oddone rightly described his study of landowners as *The Land Owning Bourgeoisie*. They were not a feudal class and never had been. They were in business to make money in the same way that the tenant farmers were. It was a question of employing their resources in the most profitable way that the circumstances of the moment permitted. The American, C. C. Taylor, who studied the rural economy of Argentina in the late 1930s and the early 1940s found that there was a mystique about landownership among tenants and owners alike, and that landownership was a goal in which nearly all believed as a great good, but that this had little effect on the drive to make money by renting in response to market forces.[12]

While there may be a case nowadays for believing that the system of landownership leads to under-utilisation of land resources, there seems to be little evidence that this was so during the years under discussion. The renting system was extremely flexible, and was a factor in the exploitation of the land without using fertilisers and without exhausting the soil. It is customary to believe that the deep humus cover of the pampas, particularly within a radius of 150 miles from Buenos Aires, made fertilisers unnecessary. In fact evidence of soil exhaustion through the too persistent cropping of wheat began to emerge in the late 1890s in the province of Santa Fe. Overall, however, there was a rough kind of rotation. Tenancies ran for 3–5 years. Cereal production was often followed by cattle finishing on alfalfa pastures, particularly in the western part of Buenos Aires province, in southern Córdoba and in the north-eastern part of San Luis. Although wheat was the biggest cash crop and the most land was devoted to wheat, the production of corn, flax, barley and oats began to develop strongly after 1900. In renting land, landowners often specified the crops tenants could plant, and few landlords were unaware of the long-term effects of persistent cropping of one kind, although they, as much as tenants, were susceptible to immediate market forces and the desire to take advantage of what seemed the most profitable line at any one moment in time.

Insufficient is known about the market in land during these years. Studies of landownership in Santa Fe for an earlier period by Ezequiel Gallo show that the holders of large tracts in that province had ceased to be holders by 1890, thus suggesting a turnover of land. Taylor found after this period, on the other hand, that the purchase of land by producers was becoming increasingly difficult. What flexibility of land use owed to buying and selling as distinct from renting is hard to assess. The list of names of large landowners presented by Oddone suggests that many who had been great owners in the time of General Rosas or earlier, such as the Anchorenas, the Alzagas, the Martinez de Hoz, were still large proprietors in 1930, but there is no scientific evidence for the impression which nevertheless exists that big proprietors also died off, disappeared and went broke in the same way as others who lacked the luck and judgement to survive in competitive conditions and in the presence of the temptation of conspicuous waste and the *dolce vita* of Buenos Aires and Paris.

The flexibility of rural industry and its responsiveness to market forces involved political and social features, the consequences of which were not noticeable so long as the overall tendencies of the world economy were favourable commercially. The predominance of tenancy did not necessarily impoverish the tenants—indeed it was the way to wealth in many instances —but it tended to impoverish rural life. Tenants on the move invested little in homes, formed few settled communities and had little interest in or concern for the development of the infrastructure of rural life: roads, schools, local government services and the means of developing a group interest with an impact on policy formation at the national level. In industrial societies rural interests have always had difficulty in making their interests known and felt, but in communities like the USA, Canada, Australia, New Zealand and France rural interests solidly based on settled communities of property-owners have been able to survive and impose on their communities policies which at least take some account of their interests. In Argentina this was so only while they encountered little real opposition from other socio-economic forces. Once the economic forces of the world ceased to operate to its advantage, the Argentine rural sector revealed little political or social capacity to look after its interests as a whole. Unlike similar interests in Australia, Canada, the United States, France and Scandinavia, the Argentine rural interests were unable to deal adequately with urban political and social pressures, which operated to their own and their country's detriment.

By 1930 the production of food and industrial raw materials by the agricultural and pastoral industries was well established in the main geographical regions of the Republic. In general the land of the sierras and the sub-tropical regions of the north and north-west produced goods consumed in Argentina itself of which there was little or no surplus for export: sugar, wine, tobacco, cotton, *yerba maté*. These regions produced cereals, cattle, sheep and goats, but, although they were additions to the national product, they were not produced in great quantities and they served to supply local and regional needs. The humid pampas, on the other hand, produced not only the cereals and meat required by the domestic market, but huge surpluses for export abroad. In 1929–30 approximately half of all agricultural production was being exported; and about 40 per cent of pastoral production. The total value of agricultural production exceeded pastoral production during the 1920s as shown in Table 6.

TABLE 6

Agricultural and pastoral production
(millions of pesos, at 1950 prices)[13]

Quinquennial averages	Agriculture	Pastoral
1920–4	4,838·9	3,885
1925–9	6,004·9	3,940

The Argentine surpluses of cereals, meat and wool for export were an important contribution to the world market for these commodities. Before World War II Argentina supplied approximately 70 per cent of the linseed, 60 per cent of the maize, 20 per cent of the wheat, 40 per cent of the chilled and frozen meat and 12 per cent of the wool in the international markets for these commodities.

The enormous production of cereals during the first thirty years of the twentieth century was achieved by an expansion of the cultivated area and an increase in the use of machinery. An absolute increase in the rural population available for work in agriculture and ranching took place from 1900 to 1914, but thereafter the increase was very small. Taylor argues that the absolute number of people in the rural sector increased only by 8,000 between 1914 and 1938, or about 1/400th of the increase in the number of town dwellers.[14] This does not agree with other calculations, but, whatever the differences of detail, there can be no mistake about the fact that substantial additions to the labour force were not a major factor in increasing totals of agricultural production. The use of machines, on the other hand, increased as shown in Table 7.

TABLE 7

Use of agricultural machinery, 1907–1930[15]

	Number of combines	Threshers	Tractors
1907–8	520	5,740	—
1914–15	1,760	5,437	
1925	—	—	6,000
1929–30	32,831	10,219	16,300

During the entire period the structure of the capital stock invested in the rural sector as a whole moved away from an emphasis on animals towards a reliance on machines. In spite of aspirations towards landownership, the tenant farmers tended to invest in machines in order to undertake large-scale production.

During these years there was some increase in productivity per hectare in wheat. A rough estimate for the years 1901–5 inclusive indicates an average production of about 730 kilograms per hectare. Between 1920 and 1929 average production was 876–879 kilograms per hectare.[6] As in much else, the tendency in the 1920s was towards a stability of productivity per unit cultivated, a state of affairs which compared favourably with the falling-off of productivity in countries like the United States where, later, productivity greatly increased after the dramatic technological breakthrough in plant breeding, plant hygiene and fertilisers.

By the turn of the century the long-established staple export, wool, had reached a peak of production which was not often exceeded in the future. If the production of wool in 1950 is taken as a norm of 100, wool production fluctuated as shown in the diagram on the opposite page.

The 200,000 tons per annum to which the norm approximated were produced from progressively fewer sheep. The census of 1908 showed a total of 67,200,000 head. This fell to a minimum of 36,200,000 in 1922. Thereafter until 1930 the total rose to 44,400,000 head.[17] The fact that a decline in numbers was not matched by a corresponding decline in the production of wool is explicable in terms of improvement in the breeding of species suitable to the environment, and the shift in the centres

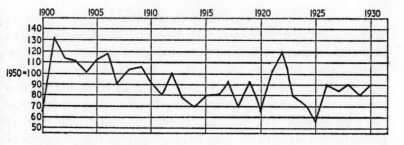

Wool production, 1900–1930 (1950 = 100)

of production away from the humid pampas to the colder, drier areas of Patagonia. In 1895 94 per cent of all sheep were raised in the areas adjacent to the river Plate, which were becoming the cereal belt. By 1930 this percentage was down to 55 per cent whereas the percentage in Patagonia had grown from 2·3 per cent to 42·6 per cent by 1930. This shift represented further specialisation.

During the first decade of the twentieth century the cattle industry underwent substantial changes. In 1900 Britain closed its ports to the importing of live cattle from Argentina and other areas where foot and mouth disease was endemic. This happened at a time of growing demand for fresh and frozen beef occasioned in part by the war in South Africa. The value of Argentine exports of frozen beef jumped from 263,000 gold pesos in 1899 to 2,459,000 gold pesos in 1900, and thereafter rose steadily to 33,205,000 gold pesos in 1913.[18] The packing houses exporting frozen meat had relied on mutton as a staple of the trade. In 1898 the value of frozen mutton exported was ten times that of beef. The trade was a hazardous and un-profitable one. The sharp increase in demand, however, altered this situation. A firm in Britain named the South African Cold Storage Company earned profits five times the invested capital in two years.[19] In accordance with their usual behaviour, investors, seeing that risks were no longer great and profits were huge, began to pour money into the frozen meat business. The expansion of the Argentine packing industry at once began to accelerate its effects upon the organisation and structure of the cattle industry.

D

The packers exporting frozen (and, after 1907) chilled beef greatly increased the demand for steers with a strongly favourable ratio of meat to bone. More and more the industry began to specialise. Breeders (or *creadores*), the more numerous and heterogeneous group, now began increasingly to supply two markets: the domestic market for beef and that of the fatteners (or *invernadores*). The breeders raised their herds on natural pastures and were to be found everywhere in the provinces of Buenos Aires, Santa Fe, San Luis and Corrientes. They were to be found, too, in Córdoba, Entre Rios and La Pampa, but these provinces had a heavier concentration of fatteners than the first group. Big breeders with large herds, permanent establishments and large investments existed side by side with small breeders with herds averaging 700 head. There were big fatteners, too, and small fatteners, but the fatteners tended to be large operators handling herds in excess of 3,000 head.[20] Breeding and fattening were businesses, whether or not the rancher had a permanent establishment and employed peons to tend his gardens and mansion or was a tenant who rented land simply to carry on a process. Neither breeders nor fatteners employed many men. It was a large and luxurious *estancia* which employed 50 men. Ten men could handle 3,000 head under the direction of a majordomo. In the 1930s peons were paid £2–£3 a month with free food and housing, and land was rented for less than £1 per hectare in breeding areas.[21] Fattening, of course, required artificial pastures, usually of alfalfa or Sudan grass, and this presupposed the preparation of pastures by renting to cereal farmers.

Although cattle raising was an important export industry, it remained, as it had long been, solidly based on a large and growing domestic market for meat. To the Argentine meat means beef, and a meatless day or week is one when the Argentine is obliged to make do on mutton, goat, pork, fish and poultry. In the years 1920–4 Argentines consumed 165lb of beef per person per year, which means that even the babes-in-arms had available to them nearly half a pound of beef a day. Not content with 165lb a year, the people were gobbling down an average of 178lb a year by 1930.[22] The national cattle herd was from two-and-a-half to three times the human population.

The production of food and raw materials by the farmers and ranchers and their marketing domestically and internationally were fundamental factors in industrial growth and the rapid development of cities. By 1914 52·7 per cent of the Argentine people lived in cities of more than 2,000 inhabitants, and approximately 20 per cent lived in Buenos Aires. 13·7 per cent of the economically active population at this time were employed in industry compared with 41·2 per cent in agriculture and ranching, and 9·1 per cent in commerce, 3·5 per cent in transport, and 32·5 per cent in services including artisanal services.[23] The 440,000 workers in industry were distributed as shown in Table 8.

TABLE 8

Distribution of industrial workers, 1914[24]

	%
Foodstuffs and beverages	34·5
Tobacco	1·8
Textiles	3·8
Clothing	10·5
Wood products	12·9
Paper and cardboard	0·8
Printing and publishing	3·1
Chemical products	2·3
Leather products	7·5
Stone, glass and ceramics	7·5
Metals	9·9
Vehicles and machinery	2·6
Electrical machines and appliances	0·8
Other manufacturing	2·3

A substantial proportion of this industry was concerned with supplying the domestic market with consumer goods. As many people were employed in sugar mills as in *frigoríficos* (14,685 and 14,687), and sugar mills supplied the domestic market, and the *frigoríficos* largely markets abroad. Shoemaking employed as many workers, and this was entirely for the domestic market. Only about 2 per cent of the production of flour mills was exported—mainly to Brazil.

Industries devoted to the production of the capital requirements of agriculture, ranching and transport were not well developed. Metal workers were the largest employment category, 23,141, in 1914, but they were not primarily producers of engineering products. The galvanised iron industry using imported sheets galvanised in Argentina and made up into roofing, tanks, buckets and bins was important. Using imported steel, hand tools, ploughs, cultivators and mowing equipment were produced, but Argentina in 1914, and even in 1930, was not manufacturing harvesting combines, tractors, railway locomotives, hoisting equipment, electric dynamos and other relatively sophisticated engineering products. This said, it must be observed, however, that by 1914 the effect of industrial growth was already noticeably affecting the character of Argentine imports from foreign countries. In 1900 imports of food, beverages, textiles, consumer durables and tobacco accounted for more than half of Argentine imports, whereas equipment for farms and ranches, railways and the public services accounted for only 10 per cent of imports, although this percentage had been as high as 30 in the late 1880s. Materials used in industry such as fuel, iron and steel, yarn and thread, chemicals and construction materials were running in the neighbourhood of 30 per cent in 1900. By 1914 this last category exceeded 50 per cent of all imports while the other two categories were declining. It was in 1910 that fuel, chemicals, iron and steel, etc first exceeded consumer goods as a proportion of total imports.[25]

The depression, which set in in 1913 followed by World War I and its aftermath, disturbed the system of Argentine economic development, and marginally changed its character. The decline in foreign capital investment, due to high interest rates in Europe, the uncertainties created by the Balkan War, growing political tension in Europe generally and a serious crop failure in Argentina itself, checked expansion and generated unemployment. This condition lasted until 1915. Thereafter exports expanded. The disruption of European supplies of cereals and meat by war increased dependence on overseas suppliers, and the trade in frozen and canned meat particularly expanded by roughly 50 per cent between 1914 and 1918. At the same time the availability and price of imports into Argentina became adverse. This was potentially an advantage to Argentine industrial development, and the trend towards more manufacturing of imported raw and semi-manufactured materials was accentuated. Cotton spinning was established. The production of chemicals for water filtering plants was begun. Petroleum production and refining were expanded. In 1916 a motor car assembly plant was opened.

When the war was over some of the advances in industrial output were lost, owing to renewed foreign competition, industrial unrest and the revival of favourable terms of trade as between rural products and imported industrial products. By 1929, however, the dependence on foreign imports was less than it had been at the beginning of the century. In 1900 all petroleum products were imported. By 1929 only 53 per cent of refined petroleum used in Argentina was imported. Metals were down from 87 per cent to 65 per cent; machinery and vehicles from 92 per cent to 79 per cent. But the limited nature of the shift was indicated by the decline from 100 per cent imported electrical equipment in 1900 to a 98 per cent dependence in 1929.[26]

Critical for the development of industry is the availability of fuel and power. In this respect Argentina suffered some handicaps. So long as coal was the principal source of heat converted into kinetic energy, Argentina was completely dependent upon imports from abroad. In terms of cost and quality, coal in South Wales or Poland was closer to the Argentine centres of production than the deposits in the Río Turbio basin in southern Patagonia. Until World War II 100 per cent of all coal consumed in Argentina was imported. In the matter of petroleum there was a much better endowment of resources. Oil was first discovered in 1907 at Comodoro Rivadavia in Patagonia. Until 1915 this was exploited as a state monopoly. Shortages of coal during World War I plus rapidly changing technology obliged the government to speed up exploitation, and private firms were admitted. In 1923 a large state-owned oil enterprise devoted to exploration, drilling, refining and marketing wholesale and retail—Yacimientos Petrolíferos Fiscales—was established under the leadership of an Argentine soldier,

General Enrico Mosconi. In 1911–15, 530 kilogrammes of coal were being consumed per head of population and 30 kilogrammes of petroleum. By 1930 the consumption was 288 kilogrammes of coal and 243 kilogrammes of petroleum;[27] over half of this was being produced in Argentina and approximately 30 per cent of it by YPF.

Electricity generation depended upon coal and oil. Water flows for the production of hydro-electricity were good but remote from the main centres of population. A hydro plant was built in Córdoba in 1898, but no efforts were made before 1930 to construct hydro plants exploiting great heads of water such as exist at Salto Grande on the Río Uruguay or at Chocón on the Río Negro. The industry of Buenos Aires and the Litoral depended entirely on thermal electric plants burning coal and oil, and this was almost the case elsewhere in the Republic. One large enterprise, Compania Argentina de Electricidad, owned by Spanish and American interests produced more than 50 per cent of all electric power, and was the principal supplier of Buenos Aires. Another foreign company owned by Swiss capitalists but called Compania Italo-Argentina de Electricidad had about 15 per cent of the market. American and Chilean companies operated numerous small plants throughout the Republic. There were also many privately owned generating plants operated by industries for their own use. These were inevitably small, low-temperature plants, with poor conversion factors of heat to energy. The use of electricity was confined almost entirely to the cities. Fifty per cent of all electricity was consumed in the Federal Capital and 75 per cent in the city and province of Buenos Aires.

The consumption of electricity was an indicator of industrial location. In 1930, 30 per cent of all industrial plants and 44 per cent of the work force were within the boundaries of the Federal Capital, and 60 per cent of the workers and 70 per cent of all factories were in the city and province of Buenos Aires, most of them within a fifty-mile radius of the Plaza San Martín at the centre of the great city. The factors in this concentration of industrial activity at this time are simple to state in terms of availability of factors of production. Labour was abundant and skilled, and Buenos Aires was a magnet which continued to draw workers from northern Italy, and from Spain. Seaborne coal and oil were available in the ports of the river Plate at the lowest prices in the Republic, and coal and oil meant electric power. Buenos Aires was, too, the metropolis of Argentina: the centre of consumption and at this time the most attractive city in the southern hemisphere. It was, therefore, a good market. In the concentration and growth of industry these factors were self-reinforcing, with the result that Buenos Aires was far and away the biggest industrial city of the nation.

In 1925 the Argentine economist and engineer Alejandro Bunge estimated that there were 61,000 industrial enterprises in the Republic employing 600,000 people working with installed motors of 1,000,000hp.[28] This suggests that enterprises were small in size. An estimate ten years later showed that only 5·6 per cent of all enterprises were joint stock companies, but that these were much larger in terms of employees than the private firms. They employed 40 per cent of the work force.[29] The vast majority of the industrial enterprises were Argentine-owned, but the majority of their proprietors in the 1920s were immigrants born in Europe.[30] Many big enterprises were foreign-owned in the sense that their shareholders and often their head offices were in Europe and the United States. Roughly 80 per cent of the *frigoríficos* were American or British. The electric supply industry was Spanish, Swiss, American and Chilean. Railways, which were big employers of metal-working mechanics, machinists and electricians, were 60 per cent foreign-owned, mainly British with a substantial minority of French capital. On the other hand, several large enterprises such as breweries (one, the second largest brewery in the world), shoe manufacturers, and textile firms were Argentine-owned. Alpargatas SA, the largest light industrial enterprise producing shoes, *alpargatas* and cotton textiles, was owned largely and controlled wholly by a third-generation Scots-Argentine family, the Frasers.

Government policy with respect to industrialisation can best be described as neutral. There are no proofs of the assertion often made that the landed interests discouraged industrialisa-

tion. Tariff protection for industry was haphazard, but it was
real. The Argentine economist C. F. Díaz Alejandro has made
a detailed study of Argentine tariffs as aids or otherwise to industrialisation. This has demonstrated the inadequacies and
contradictions of the abundant literature[31] devoted to the
argument that Argentine fiscal policy was a persistent and
deliberate disincentive to industrialisation. Díaz Alejandro has
found, for example, that output tariffs were generally higher
than import tariffs, and that some industries enjoyed tariff
protection of 100 per cent on foreign products competing with
their products. A notable and long-standing example of a protective tariff on a commodity of prime importance to the agricultural interest was that levied on jute bags. Raw jute was
admitted duty-free, but the tariff on jute fabric and made-up
jute bags was prohibitive, and the price of Argentine jute bags
was above the price of imported bags before tariff.

Díaz Alejandro further found that exchange rates of the peso
against the US dollar and the pound sterling between 1914 and
1929 were above the par of 1914, except during 1917–19 for the
dollar, and 1915–20 for the pound. At the same time the
Argentine cost of living was anything from 7 to 26 per cent less
than the cost of living in the USA or in Britain during the
1920s. High exchange rates plus low cost of living were themselves incentives to industrialisation.[32]

There was one passive but important element in the fiscal
policies of Argentina. There was in Argentina from the days of
Rosas, and, indeed, from the days of the Viceroyalty, a parallelism of interest among consumers from the top to the bottom
of society favourable to buying all consumer goods as cheaply
as possible. There was little popular sentiment on behalf of
making jobs by keeping out foreign products, and the 'full
dinner pail' argument, which in the United States made the
high tariff policies of the Republican Party in the USA popular
with industrial workers until the 1930s, had little effect in
Argentina. Even the Unión Ferroviaria, the railway workers'
union, which advocated the manufacture of railway rolling
stock in Argentina, was opposed to protective tariffs on manufactured goods.[33]

Until the advent of Peronism, the Argentine Socialist Party was the only political group devoted exclusively to voicing the interests of the wage-working class, and this party was dogmatically opposed to tariffs and protection on the grounds that they raised the cost of living of the workers. Until 1930 Argentina was, except during the upsets of World War II, a full-employment economy, with the result that real wages, not the making of jobs, was a prime concern. The tariff protection of industry and the protective consequences of exchange rates based on a gold standard were not the product of a national xenophobia or of a deliberate policy of industrialisation and were much to popular advantage, judged by real wages and the cost of living in Argentina, which was low in comparison with more industrialised countries.

By 1930 the supply of capital generated in Argentina was sufficient to have brought down interest rates to the levels prevailing in the capital markets in Europe and the United States. It was possible for public authorities and large enterprises to finance themselves as cheaply in Argentina as abroad.[34] Argentine banks had the resources to finance house-building, public works, and industrial growth. The experience of the di Tella enterprise demonstrates this. SIAM di Tella, a pioneer firm in light engineering, was started in 1911 with a capital of 10,000 pesos found from the family savings of two men, Guido Allegrucci and Torcuato di Tella. By 1927 the capital of SIAM di Tella was 3 million pesos, with net sales in the neighbourhood of 5 million pesos. This development had been financed largely by bank loans and credit sales financed by banks.[35] On the other hand, the financing of industry through the issue of share capital and debentures was not well developed. During the years 1926–9, 64 per cent of the trading on the Bueno Aires bourse was mortgage paper, 25 per cent public securities and only 11 per cent shares and debentures.[36] This is a fair indication of the extent to which capital was used to finance consumption goods like housing and public improvements rather than industrial activity. It is an indication, too, that the Argentines of this age were not yet obsessed with industrial development, and were still mainly concerned with economic

activity as a means of achieving an agreeable private and public
life.

During the years 1899–1929 tax revenues multiplied faster
than population. Public revenues in 1929 were approximately
five times what they had been at the turn of the century, and
population was roughly 2·75 times as great. As a percentage of
the gross domestic product, public expenditures tended to decline. In the years 1900–4 they had averaged 12·4 per cent, and
3·9 per cent was the proportion spent on capital borrowed by
the public authorities. In 1920–4 the percentage of public
expenditure was down to 8·8 and the percentage of outgoings
on capital was 2·6. There was an increase in the quinquennium
preceding the depression of 1929 to 10·9 per cent and 4·7 per
cent respectively, as if preparing for the take-off into expansive
public spending which has characterised the last forty years of
Argentine history.[37]

Although Argentina from the turn of the century to the 1930s
was primarily a *laissez faire* market economy in which incomes
of workers, capitalists and property-owners tended to be determined by competitive demand for the factors of production,
there were many manifestations of group interests seeking to
influence economic events to their own advantage. The open
competitive market and freedom of contract were not the sole
means of determining who sold what to whom and at what
price. There were tensions in Argentine society during the whole
of the period which, economic in origin, were not entirely re-
solved by the forces of the market but in varying degrees
depended for their management upon socio-political power
exercised by the groups themselves or by the state.

As the economy developed, more and more organisations
grew up devoted to looking after the interests of their members.
The cattlemen and landlords organised themselves in various
societies, the most prestigious being the Sociedad Rural. Industrialists organised the Unión Industrial. Artisans, wage-
workers and shopkeepers organised trade unions and mutual
benefit societies. Such organisations were not necessarily or
always engaged in protecting or advancing the economic
interests of their members in the sense of a concern with prices

or wages or the level of rents. The Sociedad Rural and other regional rural societies concerned themselves with technical matters such as the provision of stud books and the diffusion of information about ranching and meat marketing, and they served also to confer social prestige upon their members, but they also acted as a pressure group concerned with railway rates, the marketing policies of meat packers, and government action. Among immigrant workers, mutual societies devoted to caring for the sick, burying the dead and relieving distress were more common than trade unions, and the most successful and enduring trade unions incorporated in their activities social functions relating to pensions, welfare and recreation which are still strong features of Argentine trade unions.

Areas of tension between interests were to be found in almost every part of the Argentine economy: both between domestic interests and between Argentine and foreign interests and among the foreigners in Argentina. The agriculturalists and stockmen, who were the principal consumers of railway services, were from time to time dissatisfied with railway freight rates and services. Because the railways were about 80 per cent owned privately by foreign shareholders and managed at the top levels by foreigners, the railway 'problem' was frequently discussed in terms of nationalism and public ownership. If the railways belonged to the Argentines and to the state, all would be well. Newspapers like *La Nación*, which had a strong following among the educated upper class, wrote politely about nationalisation on and off for forty years. How serious this was and what were the objectives of its strictures on foreign railway proprietors may be judged by the fact that the son of the founder of *La Nación*, Ingeniero Emiliano Mitre, was able in 1907 to induce the Congress and the President to pass Law 5315, commonly known as the Mitre Law, which gave the Argentine government some general control over the railways with respect to fixing rates for goods and passengers. By 1907 some of the franchises of the railway companies had become, through change or negligence on the part of the government, extremely loose and favourable to the railway proprietors. Mitre's law did standardise franchises, but it guaranteed the railway companies some extraordinary privileges such as exemption from all taxation, municipal, provincial and national, including customs duties on imports of fuel and equipment for forty years. A 3 per cent tax on income, after the deduction of 60 per cent for expenses, was fixed for forty years, and the proceeds of this tax were committed to the building of roads planned to improve the access to stations. The state was empowered to fix rates if gross surpluses on an agreed capital exceeded 17 per cent for three years running. The law also permitted the state to expropriate railways in return for payments equal to the capital of the company plus 20 per cent. The Mitre Law could not be compared with the controls exercised over railways by the Interstate Commerce Commission in the United States or the Board of Railway Commissioners in Canada as a means of giving consumers a voice in determining transport charges. The explanation is probably the low proportion of transport costs in total costs in Argentina compared with the high proportions in North America, where long hauls were important in moving crops and stock, and the capital equipment of railways was much more costly on account of climate and terrain. The Argentine consumers of transport services were not as deeply affected by transport costs as North Americans were, in spite of the fact that railways in Argentina were not necessarily models of low-cost efficiency.

An area of tension which more specifically concerned the ranching interests than railway rates was the marketing of cattle and the export of meat. The Sociedad Rural had been from its foundation actively concerned to expand the market for meat, and its members had joined the others in pressing upon the government a policy of tax concessions for *frigoríficos* and a guarantee of profits on invested capital. Cattlemen had organised a *frigorífico* of their own, La Congeladora Argentina, which was not a success. When rapid expansion of meat exports set in after 1900 they established another freezing plant, La Blanca, which they sold out to American packing interests in 1909 at a considerable profit. The sale of the La Blanca plant represented the end of the efforts of the cattlemen to effect the export of meat by active participation in the trade through the agency of companies or producer co-operatives under their own control.

Until 1907 the packing industry was predominantly British in ownership with a minority owned and controlled by Argentine capital. In that year the American firm of Swift bought a large modern plant which had been built four years previously by an Anglo-European group of investors, the La Plata Cold Storage Company. This marked the entry of American enterprise into the meat trade on a large scale. Two years later a company controlled by the three great American meat packing firms, Swift, Armour and Morris, bought La Blanca. The Argentine cattlemen welcomed the prospect of American competition as a means of expansion, favourable pricing, and an entry into the American market for meat. The British, on the other hand, attempted to frighten them with the prospect of domination by 'the beef trust' whose wrongdoing was being extensively exposed by the American muckrakers. Some of the Argentine cattlemen took this up out of fear of price-fixing, and this set off an argument which lasted through 1909, echoed in the Argentine Congress, and led to an abortive attempt at legislative control of marketing. In fact the cattlemen benefited from competition among buyers for a period of two years. Prices of steers rose 15–7 per cent between 1908 and 1911, and packing houses began to lose money.

Exactly as the Argentine advocates of legislative control had predicted, the intense rivalry of the British and American packers ended in a price-fixing agreement and a rationing of the market among the *frigoríficos*. This rationalisation of the market was in part dictated by the character of the trade. While frozen beef and mutton accounted for the largest part of the trade, the growing part of the trade was in chilled beef. This commodity had to be moved quickly from producer to consumer. Chilled beef would remain fresh for only 40 days. The journey from the river Plate to London required 21–25 days. Any pile-up of chilled beef in London put the packer at the mercy of the wholesale butchers in England. They had either to sell, or freeze their stock and sell it at lower prices at greater expense. Either as buyers of cattle in Argentina or sellers of beef in Britain they had an interest in controlling competition and rationing the market among themselves. This they could do because the United States market was absorbing American production at prices higher than those in Britain, and Australia was too far away to supply the chilled trade. At the end of 1911 a 'pool' was established in which the American share was 41·35 per cent, the British share 40·15 per cent, and the Argentine share 18·5 per cent.[38] This 'pool' lasted until the American firm of Swift had completed the construction of a more up-to-date plant on a large scale. It then broke the agreement, and attempted to smash its rivals. The London market was swamped with chilled and frozen beef. If beef makes men aggressive, this was a suitable preparation for World War I. In every direction cries were uttered for action by governments: by the British cattle interests, by the Argentine cattle interests, by the British packing firms in Argentina, and by the Argentine Socialist Party speaking on behalf of Argentine working-class consumers. The only satisfied interests were the British consumers and the British government.

World War I was a period of comparative peace between the cattlemen and the meat packers. The chilled trade was suspended and all resources were devoted to freezing and canning. Prices rose and so did profits for the packers. The only interests to suffer from the war were the fatteners, who lost their market for high-grade chiller steers, and the packing-house workers whose real wages were eroded by high prices. The spokesmen for the fatteners in the Sociedad Rural demanded the expropriation of the packing houses. The workers went on strike and were driven back to work by detachments of Argentine marines after the US and British governments had complained about the interruption of the flow of supplies of bully beef. The aftermath of the war generated more tension than the war itself. Combined pressure of cattlemen and consumers of beef in Argentina resulted in anti-trust legislation designed to curb attempts to control prices by large packing houses.

The return of 'normalcy' saw the British and American packing interests girding for a great battle to determine which interests would gain the biggest share of the rapidly expanding market for chilled meat. In 1925 a meat war broke out between Vestey and Swift, the two biggest firms in the trade. The outcome was not a great rise in the price of cattle, but the collapse of the smaller packing firms, which either went bankrupt or ceased to export. When a truce was called in 1927 a new pool arrangement was reached which gave 54·9 per cent of the market to the Americans; 35·1 per cent to the British and 10 per cent to the Argentines. The outcome of this arrangement was a growing demand on the one hand for the expropriation of the packing companies and on the other for a policy of 'buying from those who buy from us', which was a way of expressing a preference for British interests on account of their preference for market and price stability. It was also a means of expressing the bitterness of the cattlemen against the failure of the American firms to open the American market to Argentine beef at a time when Argentines were buying more and more capital and consumer goods from the United States.

By comparison with the cattle industry, cereal production was free of tensions. Perhaps, lacking organisations such as the Sociedad Rural or Farm Bureau Federation in the USA, the grain farmers of Argentina did not have the means of expressing tension. This absence was due to the competitive character of tenant cereal farming, and the sharp focus of the cereal farmers on one activity: grabbing a maximum profit from the operation of putting in a crop and taking it off. So long as land was abundant and/or cereal prices were rising, the tenant system did not breed tensions. Not much is known about the changing character of land leases except that in the 1880s landlords were in search of tenants and colonists. By 1900, however, the cereal lands were nearing full use, and the attractions of cereal exploitation were still rising. The leases being signed by tenants in the oldest part of the wheat belt in the province of Santa Fe around 1910 were certainly hard on the tenant: 45 per cent of the crop to be delivered to the landowner in new bags purchased from a supplier designated by the lessor, threshed with machines rented from the lessor or his agent. The tenant was responsible, too, for killing pests and for planting what he was told to plant, and if he raised the four pigs allowed under the lease he had to deliver one to the landowner. By the terms of the lease the owner could void it without being actionable at law.[39] Whether leases had always been as one-sided as this is uncertain. There can be no doubt that by 1910, at least in Santa Fe, landowners had shifted most of the elements of risk and cost on to the shoulders of the tenants, and the tenants had only one alternative but to take it or leave it.

In 1911 there was a poor crop. Tenants faced 1912 with a debt burden as a result of having had to take all the risks of the business. At Alcorta in Santa Fe a school teacher, Francisco Bulzan, and a grain merchant, Angel Berjarrabal, who had been a socialist in his youth, persuaded the farmers that there was an alternative to taking it or leaving it, ie a rent strike. Strike action was taken, and the strike spread in response to *el grito de Alcorta*: the cry from Alcorta. The government embarked on arrests in an endeavour to break the strike. An Italian lawyer in Rosario, urged by a brother who was a priest in the farming areas, defended those arrested, asserted their constitutional rights and exposed their plight. A Federacíon Agraria was founded. The lawyer was assassinated. In fact the strike was a success, for landlords began negotiating leases at reduced rents. In Alcorta the landlords' share of the crop was cut to 28 per cent in new leases. This was the beginning of an interest in alternatives to free competition among cereal farmers and in political action through the agency of the Radical Party.

During the years up to 1930 there was little tension between industrial interests (apart from meat packers) and the rural interests. In this respect Argentina differed markedly from Canada, Australia and the United States, where tensions between farmers and industrialists were important factors in political life. There were, however, tensions within the industrial and transport sectors between workers and employers. Just as rising prices tended to mitigate and resolve tensions in other areas of economic life, rising real wages tended to do the same in relations between workers and employers. There had been many strikes of desperation in the cities and on the railways during the disturbed era of inflation of the late 1880s and 1890s. With the stabilisation of the currency and a renewal of investment after 1899, this type of strike died away, and began to appear again only with the inflation, rising prices and unemployment of the years 1915–21. In 1919 a strike in the metalworking industry for a 20 per cent increase in wages to meet the rising cost of living led to a violent confrontation between the strikers and the government. Responding to anti-Bolshevik propaganda, the Radical government of President Yrigoyen used troops and there were serious casualties among the strikers, remembered as *La Semana Tragica*. The restoration of stability saw a diminution of strikes of desperation, although the bitterness remained as a poison for the future.

During these years there was significant but uneven growth in trade unions. The predominance of small-scale enterprises of an artisanal type was an obstacle to the development of trade unions in many branches of industry, but in the railways, shoe manufacturing, the textile industry and the printing trades, unions were solidly established. By 1925 La Fraternidad, and the Unión Ferroviaria were strong institutions which organised the locomotive drivers and the railway staff. They were not only negotiating agents of the railway workers, but mutual aid societies providing medical services, pensions and a social life for their members. In the 1920s white-collar workers in banks and commercial firms organised themselves successfully along trade union/mutual society lines.

Along with capital and labour, Argentina imported from Europe ideologies. To the well-established liberalism and anti-clericalism were added socialism, anarchism, anti-Semitism and ultramontanism. Of these ideological trends only anarchism and socialism had any impact on the economy during the years 1899–1929, and that is hard to measure. Anarchism was a cultural preference of Italian and Spanish workers like spaghetti and paella. Socialism came in with the Germans, and was domesticated in Argentina by Juan B. Justo, a young, upper-class intellectual who founded and led the Socialist Party until his death in 1928. Of the two ideological trends, anarchism and socialism, the latter had the more immediate positive impact economically. The Socialists were willing to work within the framework of the liberal constitution. After the passage of the

Saenz Peña Law in 1912, which made voting compulsory and elections honest, the Socialists were the only voice in the Congress speaking in favour of benefits for the poor and unprivileged. The Socialists corrected such injustices as the practice of supplying water to workers' tenements at so much per litre measured by water meters while supplying it in unlimited amounts at flat rates to middle- and upper-class householders. Thus the Socialists aroused the conscience of society, which is so easily stilled in the presence of the growth and abundance of a market economy, and they established the vocabulary of class-struggle politics. Justo christened the landlords 'the oligarchy' and he taught the people the moral dignity of social envy. Socialists, too, encouraged collective bargaining as a legitimate form of the bargaining processes of liberal capitalist society, and fought against those who interpreted freedom of contract as a device for rendering the labour market more competitive than other markets.

The anarchists, on the other hand, were root-and-branch fanatics who wanted to wipe out the employing classes and destroy all forms of government. Because syndicates of workers were the only form of social organisation which might be allowed to survive the final revolution, they paid some attention to trade unions—usually to their detriment. Anarchists had a considerable influence in the two central organisations of trade union which developed before World War I: the Federación de Obreros Regionales Argentina and the Unión General de Trabajadores, with the result that both of these organisations refused to co-operate with the government in establishing orderly procedures for wage bargaining and the settlement of disputes between workers and employers. Extra to trade union activity was the anarchists' direct violence against the state and the upper classes. They planted bombs in the Teatro Colon, attempted to assassinate several presidents, and did succeed in assassinating the police chief of Buenos Aires in 1909. The government replied with the Law of Residence of 1902 and the Law of Social Defence of 1910 which empowered the government to deport anarchists, suspected anarchists and white slavers without trial or hearing.

While severe and uncompromising in matters of disorder and violence, the public authorities were not uniformly hostile to trade unions or to the establishment of minimum wages, holidays with pay and laws governing hours of work, the employment of minors, and the setting of standards of sanitation and hygiene in factories and shops. In 1907 they sided with the trade unions in a railway strike on the Western Railway, and forced the railway to accept arbitration. This was a step in the direction of strengthening the disposition of railway employers to negotiate with genuine trade unions instead of resorting to strong-arm tactics and the establishment of company unions. Bit by bit, and particularly after the great and violent clash in 1919, business unionism—ie collective bargaining within the framework of liberal, capitalist norms—began to triumph. In 1926 La Fraternidad, the Unión Ferroviaria and the Municipal Workers Union formed a central organisation, the Confederación Obrera Argentina, which spoke for over 100,000 wageworkers.

Notes to this chapter are on pp 194–5

7

The response to crisis,
1929-1939

Measured in terms of 1950 US dollars the purchasing power of
Argentine exports during the years 1925-9 had reached a height
never achieved before or since—$1,982·3 million. As the winter
of 1929 in Argentina wore on, the signs of the catastrophic decline of 30 per cent or more in overall purchasing power regard-
less of volume began to appear. The Argentine government and
economic leaders had no means of knowing at that time that the
Argentine economy was facing a fundamental crisis, and that
its international environment was about to undergo a profound
transformation. Their response to the economic and commercial events of 1929 was drastic enough in the light of their
immediate past policies, but, judged in the light of a longer
Argentine tradition, the decision of 16 December 1929 to end
the gold exchange standard for domestic purposes was conventional. It was assumed that a paper currency would lead to
easier credit beneficial to the rural sector and by that means
paper receipts would rise faster than costs. But this did not
happen. Wholesale prices of rural products moved as follows
(1939 = 100):[1]

1928—130		1932— 71	
1929—123		1933— 68	
1930—103		1934— 85	
1931— 76			

None the less, the Argentine pursued its traditional strategy
of endeavouring to increase receipts from sales abroad by pour-

ing more products onto the market. In 1931 export earnings from cereals were 4·2 per cent greater than in 1930 in spite of a fall of 24·4 per cent in prices. Something had, however, gone wrong, and how serious this was became increasingly evident. The terms of trade had turned heavily against Argentina. In 1925–9 $1,000 of Argentine exports at 1950 prices purchased $1,253 of imports at 1950 prices: by 1930–4 they purchased only $829.[2] Paper currency for domestic purposes might contribute to a high level of economic activity and limit unemployment, but at what cost in terms of real income for the community? Between 1930 and 1934 aggregate output, as distinct from output in the rural sector supplying the export market, fell by 14 per cent.[3] It could further be argued that a strategy of selling abroad regardless of price was aggravating the overall situation by adding to the surpluses of primary products, which, for reasons that no Argentine action could affect, were increasingly unsaleable at prices capable of covering costs.

In September 1930, the elected President of the Republic was overthrown by a military coup. From this date until December 1931, when an election carefully managed by established interests installed President Augustin Justo in office, political instability and uncertainty added to the difficulties of the country. Abroad the economic environment was changing more drastically than at any time in Argentine history. The epoch of flexible, open international trading was coming to an end. In October 1930, at an Imperial Conference, the Canadians had demanded of Britain a preferential tariff designed to protect Canadian wheat sales in Britain. This had been rejected, but, like the Smoot-Hawley Tariff Act of the previous June passed by the Congress of the United States, the Canadian demand was an indication that the great trading nations of the world were moving towards policies of economic autarchy and bilateral trading. In August 1931, a national government was formed in Britain dedicated to saving the past, which it promptly began to destroy. In September, Britain abandoned the gold standard and the sterling par of one pound to US $4.86 fell to $3.49. Being a debtor nation Argentina derived some benefit from this, but none the less serious dangers threatened. Following the election which gave enormous support to the national government in Britain, the British abandoned any further pretence of free trade. Of particular concern to Argentina was the establishment of a new kind of corn law in Britain which guaranteed British farmers a floor price for wheat well above the world price. This did not mean the closing of one of Argentina's markets, but it did bring to an end the competitive system which had enabled the producers of cheap cereals like Argentina bit by bit to destroy British cereal production. Next on the agenda was meat.

The end abroad of what can loosely be called *laissez faire* produced in Argentina a system of state management of the economy which has grown progressively more complex and particular. The central mechanism of management was a cleverly designed piece of administrative machinery called La Comisión de Control de Cambios, or Exchange Control Commission. It was created by a decree of the Executive Powers of 10 October 1931, an indication in itself that the élite who arranged the election of President Justo a few months later were already in power with a clear policy designed to meet the difficult circumstances in which Argentina found itself.

The *modus operandi* of the commission was simple. In order to obtain loading certificates exporters of Argentine produce were obliged to sell to the authorised banks acting on behalf of the commission the foreign currency obtained from the sale of produce abroad. The buying rate of the commission was pegged at 15 pesos to the pound sterling. A few 'non-regular' exports and exports to Uruguay, Bolivia, Chile, Peru and Paraguay were exempt from the requirement, and in this way a small 'free' market was allowed to exist parallel to the controlled market.

The foreign exchange purchased by the commission was then used in accordance with a list of priorities. The first claim on the stock of foreign exchange was the government's requirement to meet interest and sinking fund charges on the debt held abroad. After the needs of the federal, provincial and municipal governments on account of debt service were met, the commission auctioned the remaining foreign exchange for purchases abroad in accordance with a list of priorities as follows:[4]

1. Raw materials needed for national industries
2. Fuel
3. Indispensable consumer goods
4. Remissions home by immigrants
5. Remissions to Argentine citizens resident abroad
6. Travellers' expenses
7. Inessential goods
8. Liquidation of commercial debts

The price of foreign exchange established by auction fluctuated between 16·44 and 17·44 to the pound sterling. In January 1936, 17 was fixed as the selling price. The free market was theoretically a limited one, but there were leakages from the controlled to the free market, so much so that the free market was responsive to the conditions of international trade. In December 1936, for example, the prospect of a good crop and an improvement in prices generated so much foreign exchange that the peso strengthened on the free market to 16 to the pound, and the commission raised the price of the peso to 17. On the other hand the free peso fell to 20·62 to the pound on the free market in November 1938, following a crop failure.[5]

The spread between the buying rate and the selling rate yielded a profit to the commission. The designated purposes of the profit were, firstly, to help the state bear the cost of servicing the public debt held abroad and, secondly, after Federico Pinedo became finance minister in 1933, to provide a price support fund for a Grain Commission established by him.

On the eve of the great depression Argentina was exporting approximately 40 per cent of its production and importing approximately 36 per cent of its consumption. The establishment of control over the foreign exchanges meant, therefore, the creation of a very powerful instrument of economic management both of the domestic economy and of the foreign trade of the nation. The commission in fact had the power to tax, inasmuch as it acquired spendable resources by making a profit out of buying foreign exchange at a pegged price and selling it at a price determined wholly or in part by itself. Its receipts, however, differed from treasury receipts inasmuch as they were

used for specific economic and commercial purposes which
were not determined by a public political process. The side
effects of the commission's activities were often as important for
economic development as its intentions.

As to its conscious intentions these were primarily two: to
maintain the credit rating of Argentina in the capital markets
of the world, and to preserve as far as possible its markets overseas. These were essentially traditional and conservative purposes, and only the techniques for their realisation were new.
Maintenance of the credit rating of the Republic, of course,
meant the continued payment of interest and sinking fund
charges on the debts of the public authorities and other institutions such as railway companies, electricity supply companies
and so on which had obtained capital through borrowing by
way of bonds and debentures. With the severe fall in prices the
relative cost of debt service mounted. Beveraggi Allende, an
Argentine economist, has invented a coefficient of indebtedness,
and he calculated that between 1927 and 1933 the Argentine
coefficient of indebtedness rose from 18 per cent to 38 per cent.[6]
The Exchange Commission met this increased burden by taxing
the exporting interests, ie the rural sector of the economy. As a
result of maintaining the Argentine credit rating in a world of
repudiation the commission got the coefficient of indebtedness
down to pre-depression levels by 1937 through discharge of
debts and funding at lower rates of interest. Additional to this
in reducing the debt burden was the depreciation of sterling and
the US dollar, the improvement in the prices of Argentine
exports and the improvement of the Argentine share in the
world cereal markets as a result of good crops in Argentina and
bad ones in Canada and the United States. Whether the effort
made to maintain the Argentine credit rating in the capital
markets was worthwhile in terms of economic development is
open to question, but there is no doubt that the preservation of
Argentine credit was closely linked with the maintenance of
Argentine markets abroad.

The developments of the 1920s had created a problem for
Argentina which was soluble so long as there was something
approximating to a free flow of goods and services in inter-

national trade. This problem centred around the fact that during the 1920s Argentina began to increase its purchases of goods manufactured in the United States, but was not increasing its sales in the United States. In 1913–14 Britain was supplying 31·3 per cent of Argentine imports, the United States 14·3 per cent, Germany 16·7 per cent, France 9·4 per cent, and Italy 8·5 per cent. During World War I the American share grew, but in 1922 it was 22·1 per cent and the British share 23·5 per cent. Thereafter, the American share increased and the British diminished, so that by 1929 the Americans had 26·3 per cent of the Argentine market, the British 18·6 per cent, the Germans 11·5 per cent, the French 6·1 per cent and the Italians 8·8 per cent.[7] On the other hand, Britain and the European states were Argentina's best markets by a long way. In 1929 Britain took 31·5 per cent of Argentine exports and the European continent 43 per cent. The United States, on the other hand, took only 9·4 per cent of Argentina's exports.[8] Some of the obstacles to trade with the United States were man-made. The American *ad valorem* tariff on combing wool, a prime Argentine export, was 60·8 per cent in 1929; on carpet wool 24·2 per cent; on linseed, 26·8 per cent; and chilled and frozen meat were prohibited under sanitary regulations.[9] As prices fell during the depression these tariff obstacles became higher in terms of percentages of value. The tariff on combing wool was 150 per cent in 1935 and the tariff on linseed was 74.9 per cent.

The American determination to sell without buying, which is what their tariff policy amounted to, was a possible pattern of participation in international commerce as long as the Americans were willing and able to lend money on a large scale. Both willingness and ability came to an end in the autumn of 1929. The way out for communities like Argentina, greatly dependent on foreign trade for economic wellbeing, seemed to lie in the direction of bilateral trading arrangements governed by treaties. Before the depression struck, interests in Argentina and in Britain had developed the slogan 'buy from those who buy from us', and in 1929 a British economic mission headed by Lord D'Abernon visited Argentina. He reached an agreement with the Argentine authorities, the object of which was to make operative the 'buy from us' slogan by establishing a line of credit generated by Argentine sales in Britain which was to be available only for the purchase of British goods. The agreement never came into operation, but it contained within it the seeds of a system of bilateralism which developed strongly as the depression deepened, and which in the end bound Argentina to the main trading nations of western Europe. Although the Roca-Runciman agreement between Britain and Argentina signed in 1933 is the best known and most discussed bilateral agreement signed by Argentina, it was not the first such agreement, nor was it the only one. In August 1931, Argentina signed an agreement with Finland which bound her to buy Finnish birch plywood free of duty in return for a Finnish undertaking to buy bran and certain cereal milling by-products free of duty. By 1937 Argentina had bilateral trading and exchange agreements with Belgium, Luxembourg, Germany, the Netherlands, Spain, France, Italy, Rumania, and Austria as well as with her neighbours in South America, Uruguay, Brazil and Peru.[10]

The Roca-Runciman agreement[11] merits more attention than the other bilateral trading agreements not only because it involved a very large and important trade, but because it serves to illustrate the nature of Argentina's trading problems once her best customers began to restrict the free sale of primary products. The overwhelming victory of the national government in the British elections of October 1931 involved a commitment on the part of the dominant partners in the coalition of Conservatives, National Liberals and National Labour to policies of national protection and imperial preference in trade. Manufactured goods were already protected, and in February 1932 the Wheat Act marked the beginning of protection for food producers. In August 1932, at an imperial conference in Ottawa, the British and Commonwealth governments agreed to raise duties against the rest of the world, and to ease, or at least not increase, the barriers to trade among the nations and colonies of the British Empire. In particular the preferences given to Canada, Australia, New Zealand and South Africa were bound to affect the Argentine position in the British market for meat, wool and cereals.

The Argentine government itself had already embarked on a policy of protecting its markets. In February 1931, import duties were imposed on all fresh and refrigerated fruits, vegetables and fish. This hit the American export of apples and pears to Argentina. A comprehensive increase in duties and valuation lists was applied to beverages and foodstuffs, cotton and woollen textiles and yarns, leather and leather goods, hats and caps, cement, motion picture films, typewriters and calculating machines. Surtaxes were imposed on tools made of iron and steel, thread, rice and rubber goods.

When Vice-President Julio Roca led his delegation to London both Argentina and Britain were in a position to negotiate. Both parties had market opportunities to offer the other. Britain as a creditor had claims on Argentina, and the Argentine government through its Exchange Control Commission had control of the foreign exchange with which these claims could be met. The result was a deal. Britain guaranteed Argentina a place in the British market for meat at a proportion less than in the past, but still at a level only 10 per cent below that prevailing at the time of the negotiation. Britain further agreed to assist its farmers with subsidies on cereals and not by way of tariff and quota controls limiting access to the market. Argentina, for its part, undertook to stabilise its tariffs, to reduce some and to guarantee the free import of coal. As for the payment of debts it undertook to release the necessary foreign exchange, and to consider favourably applications for remittances from Argentina so long as it had foreign exchange generated by sales in Britain. Following the agreement and in order to implement it the Argentine government by a decree of 28 November 1933 empowered the Exchange Control Commission to require importers and others desiring foreign exchange to obtain permits to purchase foreign exchange, and the granting of these permits was left to the decision of the commission. As far as one can judge from the trade figures, the agreement worked as intended. Surveying the quinquennium before the outbreak of World War II the British Department of Overseas Trade was able to say: 'The United

Kingdom official trade returns show that during the five years immediately preceding the outbreak of war in 1939 United Kingdom exports maintained a high level.'[12] Relative to the US the position of Britain in the Argentine market had improved by 1938 to a 20 per cent share compared with a 17·3 per cent share for the United States.[13]

While the response of the Argentine government and economic leaders to the challenge of depression was designed to conserve the economy created in the previous half-century or more, it cannot on that account be despised. Compared with nations like the USA and Canada the Argentine response to depression measured in terms of the gross domestic product was very good. In 1939 the Argentine GDP was nearly 15 per cent above that of 1929 and 33 per cent better than the GDP in 1932, whereas the increase in the US was only 4 per cent and the Canadian increase was a similarly small percentage.[14] The collection of data on unemployment in Argentina did not begin until 1935, but the literary evidence of its existence contained in newspapers and journals suggests that this problem in no way resembled the massive unemployment characteristic of the United States, Great Britain or Canada. The comparatively small scale of the unemployment may, of course, have owed less to good economic management than to the comparatively simple nature of the Argentine economy which still lacked industries dependent for their activity on capital investment or affected adversely by serious declines in consumer demand. The consequences of decline in investment in Argentina and the contraction of the consumption function there tended to be felt more outside Argentina, an advantage of the economy in the days of the oligarchy which is either forgotten or unknown to the modern enthusiasts for intense industrialisation.

If the conservation of the rural-export economy was one of the objectives of the economic policy-makers, another was its diversification and the correction of some of its weaknesses. When the Exchange Control Commission was established it had been intended that the profits from foreign exchange dealings should be used to assist agriculture and ranching. At first most of the profits were applied to debt service but this use declined, as shown in Table 9.

TABLE 9

Exchange profits used for debt service (millions of pesos)[15]

	Exchange profits	Used for debt service
1933	0·4	0·4
1934	23·9	22·3
1935	43·2	34·9
1936	33·0	27·3
1937	25·4	18·9
1938	33·5	16·8
1939	34·1	17·8
1940	31·4	16·0

More and more of these surpluses, which were a form of forced saving, were applied to strengthening the rural sector by creating facilities and guarantees which private investment had not provided, eg more and better dispersed grain elevators and storage space, a stabilisation of expectations in the shape of floor prices which, when the war came, was converted to a policy of government purchase. The exchange control was used to encourage the production and export of fruit and vegetables, both fresh and canned. Tea and cotton growing were encouraged. Minimum sugar prices were guaranteed. The cultivation of oil seeds and fodder crops was promoted. Tax exemptions were given to farmers paying rent of less than 3,000 pesos a year or working farms of their own valued at less than 30,000 pesos. All this represented an attempt at increased rationality in organising production and a necessary and welcome departure from the happy-go-lucky dependence on the bounty of nature and favourable terms of international trade which had for too long characterised Argentina's approach to its principal source of wealth. It represented, too, an attempt to bring some relief and support to cereal farmers, whose economic importance was not matched by social prestige and political influence. Compared with the United States and Canada where farming contracted and declined during the 1930s, Argentine farming grew and improved technologically. The cultivated area grew from 26·7 million hectares in 1929–30 to 28·4 million hectares in 1939–40, and the number of tractors used from 16,220 to 23,540 and of harvesters from 28,656 to 42,729.[16]

Some attention, too, was paid to the improvement of the rural infrastructure. The roads of Argentina were notoriously bad. The absence of gravel and stone on the pampas and the extensive nature of private estates were obstacles to the construction of satisfactory all-weather roads in the main areas of production. The road building programme provided for under the Mitre Law of 1907 was designed to improve access to railways, not to create an arterial system for the use of motor vehicles. In 1931 duties on crude oil and diesel oil were removed and in 1933 a highway-building programme was inaugurated. By 1939 all the main centres of Argentina were connected by all-weather, hard-surface highways. Unfortunately the expansion of the road system was not matched by the growth of the number of motor vehicles. The number of motor cars and lorries per head of population was lower in 1940 than it was in 1930, and the absolute numbers were less, 435,822 in 1930 compared with 427,750 in 1940, but the number of vans and lorries was 27 per cent greater.[17]

The Exchange Control Commission and the various organisations such as the Grain Commission, the National Meat Board, the Quebracho Commission and so on, which ramified from this endeavour to manage the economy, were not the only mechanisms of more particular, centralised direction designed and developed in the 1930s. In 1935 a Central Bank was established, which took over the functions of the Caja de Conversion, and became the holder of the gold and currency reserves of the nation, the lender of last resort available to the commercial banks and the sole note-issuing bank. The suspension of free convertibility in 1929, and the pegging of the peso to currencies like the pound sterling and the US dollar, both of which were devalued in terms of gold, meant that Argentina had itself devalued its currency. The establishment of the Central Bank was an opportunity formally to revalue the nation's gold reserves in terms of the paper currency. The gold holdings of the

Caja de Conversion were revalued at 0·2929 grammes of fine
gold per paper peso as compared with 0·6397 grammes. This
represented a devaluation of 54·213 per cent compared with the
pre-1929 figures. The paper profits on the revaluation of gold
stocks were of the order of 700,000,000 pesos. These were distributed to the Banco de la Nacion, owned by the state and engaged in ordinary banking operations, and to other banks.
There was thus no sudden injection of currency into the system.
As a consequence, internal prices remained stable. Observers
have remarked on the extraordinary stability of Argentine
domestic prices compared with those of other important economic communities during the 1930s. The lowest point was 82
(1926 = 100) reached in 1933 compared with 62 in the United
States.[18]

The financial policies of the Argentine government were
prudently designed to calm the nerves of the public and to induce stability of expectations. Expenditure exceeded revenue in
only five of the ten years between 1931 and 1940 inclusive, and
then only by small amounts. If the profits of the Exchange Control Commission are included in the public revenues, there were
deficits in 1931 and 1932 only. On the other hand, the Argentine government spent money on public works and after 1935 on
armaments. These were financed out of public loans floated in
Argentina. Between 1931 and 1941 the public debt of the
Republic increased by 1,926,000,000 pesos or 54 per cent. In
terms of the burden on the public revenues, however, the cost
of borrowing was kept down. In 1931 29·6 per cent of the
public revenue was absorbed by debt service. In 1941 the
absorption was only 26·7 per cent. Most important, however,
was the fact that public works and armaments were financed
out of real spending power generated in the community by the
use of land, labour and capital. Their costs were met from real
taxes which transferred real spending power from the individual
or corporation to the state; from profits from the control of
foreign exchange generated by real economic activity; and
finally by loans which represented a choice by individuals or
corporations to invest rather than to hoard or to buy consumer
goods. No one was deceived and cheated by issues of paper

currency representing nothing but the decision of the government to print pesos.

In spite of the brilliance of the government's economic strategy of conservation in the presence of revolutionary changes in the external environment, the dynamic factors in economic development were being transformed. The flow of immigrants and capital from abroad slowed down and all but ceased with the onset of depression. Net immigration, which had amounted to 1,120,000 during the years 1901–10 and 856,000 between 1921 and 1930, fell to 204,000 during the years 1931–40, and would probably have been much lower had it not been for political persecution in Europe.[19] The influx of capital from abroad fell, too, although this is hard to measure. The proportion of foreign capital in aggregate fixed capital, which had been 47·7 per cent in 1913 and 32 per cent in 1929, fell to 20·4 per cent in 1940.[20] The sources of growth were becoming more and more indigenous.

Although industrial growth was not an explicit goal of the economic leadership of the country in the way that safeguarding and strengthening the rural sector was, the consequence not only of the changes in the terms of trade but of the controls exercised by the government was a growth of industry during the 1930s. Between 1932 and 1939 value added by manufacturing grew by 62 per cent.[21] Between 1925–9 and 1935–9 the gross domestic product increased by 20 per cent, and a large part of this growth was due to increased industrial production.

The general advantage of employment of resources in non-agricultural and pastoral activities as compared with the traditionally profitable rural sector can be inferred from a look at comparative wholesale prices as shown in Table 10.

To this 'natural' advantage there was added the side effects of the policy of economic, commercial and exchange control. The term 'side effects' is used deliberately because the intention of the economic managers was not explicitly industrialisation, as it was later to become. The system of priorities in the sale of foreign exchange to importers had the effect of a tariff reinforcing existing price differentials between agricultural goods and the imported products of industry. Fuel and raw materials,

TABLE 10

Wholesale prices, 1926–1940 (1926 = 100)[22]

	Rural goods	Non-rural goods
1926	100	100
1928	109	94
1930	86	94
1931	64	94
1932	59	98
1933	57	93
1934	71	106
1935	72	104
1936	87	103
1937	105	114
1938	91	109
1939	84	115
1940	80	135

for example, had a high priority with the administrators of the exchange controls, and 'non-essential' consumer goods a low priority. Furthermore, importers were obliged to pay cash inasmuch as commercial arrears had a low priority for foreign exchange. Of course, the operation of the controls had the effect of directing the import trade from the USA to Britain and other countries having bilateral trading and exchange agreements with Argentina. The import, for example, of coal and textiles, which were British trade staples, kept up, whereas the import of motor cars, which were American exports, remained static, and the import of passenger vehicles actually fell. The increase in industry in Argentina was considerable. The percentage of imports in a number of lines of industrial as well as natural products fell during the 1930s. For example 65 per cent of the cement used in Argentina was imported in 1925–9. By 1935–9 only 5 per cent was imported. Cotton textiles fell from 92 per cent to 61 per cent. There are no data for comparison, but the statistics for 1935–9 show that 30 per cent of the rayon concerned was manufactured in Argentina, 52 per cent of the cardboard, and 25 per cent of the woodpulp and cellulose.[23]

While the industrial growth of the 1930s was impressive, its

E

character must be noted. It was a growth which did not involve
as heavy an investment of capital as that which had taken place
in the previous decades. In 1905–9 fixed investment was absorbing 45·4 per cent of available goods and services, and in
1925–9 32·9 per cent. This fell to 23·5 per cent in 1930–4 and to
24·4 per cent in 1935–9.[24] Comparatively little capital was going
into capital-intensive industry or into the infrastructure, and
most of it into the production of consumption goods. Real
consumption in fact grew by 28 per cent in the 1930s.

Industry in 1939 was still predominantly small-scale industry.
According to an estimate made by the Ministry of Finance,
there were in 1939 53,927 establishments employing 710,850
people of whom 619,721 were wage workers.[25] This estimate
was lower than subsequent estimates of the industrial population and appears to have ignored the unemployed and casual
labour. None the less, it points to numerous small establishments. On the other hand, large establishments were growing,
although very slowly. The census of 1939 showed that the percentage of establishments employing fewer than 50 workers had
declined between 1935 and 1939 from 41 to 40·1 per cent, and
the percentages of establishments with 51–500 workers and
more than 500 workers had increased slightly.[26]

In terms of production, much the biggest industry in 1930
was still meat packing. This industry accounted for roughly 15
per cent of industrial production. The next largest industry,
construction, produced about 10 per cent, the electric power
industry about 6½ per cent and the petroleum industry about 5
per cent. Several important inferences can be drawn from
statistics of production. Railway repair shops produced more
than the metallurgical industry including iron and steel: 97
million pesos compared with 77 million pesos. The assembly of
motor cars and lorries accounted for 107 million pesos of production but the servicing of motor vehicles and the manufacture
of spare parts accounted for 77 million pesos of production.
Yarn and textiles of wool and cotton were nearly as important
in terms of production as flour milling and the handling and
processing of cereals. The production of books, periodicals and
newspapers was a big industry in Argentina then as it still is,

and added more to total production than oil refining or the textile industry.

What distinguished Argentine industry in 1939 from the industry of a country of recent settlement like Canada was the absence of a capital goods industry and a motor industry. Argentina in 1939 was importing 95 per cent of its sheet steel, all of its heavy electric generators, 95 per cent of its caustic soda, 83 per cent of its electric batteries, and all of its petrol-driven motor components. Statistics of machine tool production were not even kept.

Another feature of Argentine industry in the 1930s, which must not be obscured by attending only to growth rates, was the persistently low level of technology indicated by the relatively small use of electric power. In 1939 Argentina generated 2,054,623,000kwh of electricity. Of this 43 per cent was used in industry, ie 895,776,000kwh used by 711,000 workers. This was approximately 1,250kwh per worker. This was half the consumption of electricity per worker in Germany or Britain and a quarter the consumption in the United States and Canada at that time.

Industrial development as it took place in the 1930s served to intensify the concentration of wealth and economic activity in the Litoral and particularly in the city and province of Buenos Aires. In 1939, 75 per cent of all industrial production took place in the province of Buenos Aires, and if the province of Sante Fe is added the percentage is 83·9. The production of electric power per head of population in 1940 was 640·7kwh in the city of Buenos Aires, 142·8kwh per head in the province of Buenos Aires (exclusive of the city), and 142·6kwh in the province of Santa Fe. In none of the other Argentine provinces did the production of electric power exceed 100kwh per head, and in all but Córdoba, San Juan, Mendoza and Santa Cruz it did not exceed 50kwh per inhabitant.

Generalisations about the underdevelopment or non-development of key 'modern' industries like the chemical industry, iron and steel and intermediate and advanced engineering must not be carried too far. The production and refining of petroleum in Argentina was developing satisfactorily. The leading petroleum

E*

enterprise was not only Argentine in its personnel and direction, but was a state enterprise, Yacimientos Petrolíferos Fiscales. Between 1929 and 1943 YPF increased output at an annual rate of 8·2 per cent, and it enlarged its share of the market. It has been alleged that its growth was hampered by the policy of the Exchange Control Commission, which made it difficult to obtain foreign exchange for the purchase of American oil drilling and refining equipment.[27] The allegation, however, ignored the fact that there were other suppliers besides the Americans and further that YPF, which had a good research and development department, was itself a seller of 'know how' to foreign oil companies.[28] By 1939 YPF was one of the biggest and most successful petroleum enterprises in South America, and the only one owned and operated by Latin Americans capable of executing the whole process of production from exploration to retail selling.

Between 1929 and 1939 the population increased from 11,592,000 to 13,948,000. Only 10 per cent of this increase was the result of net immigration. In 1925–9 the economically active population had been on average approximately 4,300,000. By 1935–9 this figure was 5,000,000. In 1925–9 the percentage engaged in agricultural and pastoral production had been approximately 36 per cent. By 1935–9 this had fallen slightly to 35 per cent. During the same time the percentage in industry had grown from 20·7 per cent to 22·1 per cent. Personal service still accounted for the same percentage of people—about 13·1 per cent. Commerce and finance had grown from 11·5 to 13·4 per cent and government employment from 5·1 per cent to 5·9 per cent. Construction was down from slightly less than 5 per cent to slightly more than 3 per cent.[29]

Any precise answer to a question about what kind of life the economic activity of the 1930s yielded to the Argentine people is beset with many difficulties, principally the absence of data. We know that Colin Clark, writing in 1940 on the basis of data collected for the period 1925–34, placed Argentina among the nations like the United States, Great Britain, Canada and Switzerland with a high standard of living. A comparative study of twelve countries in 1950 still showed the Argentine standard of living as high compared with Chile or Italy, but below Norway and Germany and only about one-third the level of the United States.[30] It is pretty safe to say that comparatively speaking the Argentines were 'well-off' in the 1930s, and this is further suggested by the fact that, after a near cessation of immigration in 1932–3, Europeans still immigrated to Argentina. Who were 'well-off' is harder to determine. In Buenos Aires and Mar del Plata there was, as there still is, much evidence of luxury and conspicuous consumption. How much luxury and conspicuous consumption on the part of the rich and the middle classes contributed to the general propensity of the Argentine community towards high consumption is not clear. Judged by the disposition of total goods and services available in the economy, the years 1930–9 witnessed an upward movement in consumption and a decline in investment, particularly private investment. In 1925–9 personal consumption was absorbing 60·2 per cent of goods and services and the state 6·7 per cent. Private investment was at the same time absorbing 28·3 per cent and public investment 4·6 per cent. During the worst years of the depression, 1930–4, personal consumption rose to 67·9 per cent and state consumption to 8·3 per cent, whereas private investment fell sharply to 18·6 per cent while public investment rose slightly to 4·9 per cent. During the late 1930s personal consumption dropped slightly and so did private investment. Consumption and investment by the state both rose by better than 1 per cent.[31]

Who were doing all this consuming is not clear. We do know, however, from published data that living conditions in the cities, and particularly the cities of the Litoral, were much better than in the rural areas, particularly in the west and north-west. An Argentine student of social conditions wrote:

In terms of culture, health conditions and living standards in general the rural communities of Argentina are in a state of immense inferiority and disequilibrium compared to the urban population of the republic. There are provinces in which the rural population is being consumed by anaemia, resulting from a lack of sufficient food, as well as by malaria and other diseases.[32]

Statistics of infant mortality suggest a sharp difference in living conditions between Buenos Aires and the rest of the country. In 1930 the infant mortality for the country as a whole was 100 per thousand live births under one year, but the figure for Buenos Aires was only 70 per thousand. This differential had widened by 1935 to 107:52, but had narrowed by 1940 to 87:48.[33]

Food occupied a big place in the Argentine standard of living. They were the biggest consumers of meat in the world. The Argentines ate an incredible 300lb of meat per head of population. This was more than double the consumption in Britain or the United States or Canada, and exceeded by nearly 50 per cent the consumption in Australia. Only the French and the Italians ate more bread and rice than the Argentines, and nobody drank as much coffee, tea and *yerba maté*. They were average consumers of wine and beer, but they drank a lot of milk, although not so much as the Danes, the Americans or the Swiss. They were big eaters of fruit, but they consumed comparatively few vegetables: only about one-ninth as much as the French and one-fifth as much as the Americans. Like the Italians, the Argentines did not have much taste for butter, and they were not the world's greatest eaters of cheese. They ate only 72lb of sugar a year compared with the 110lb a year consumed by the British.[34] These estimates of average food consumption were made by Carl Taylor, an American geographer, who travelled 20,000 miles through rural Argentina in 1942. Compared with the study made by the United Nations some years later, he appears to have over-estimated the consumption of meat by about 50 per cent,[35] but in general his figures agree with other indications of high food consumption, and justify his observation that he found no evidence except in very arid areas and among people working on a sugar and tea plantation of inadequate food. He observed that in the rural areas people ate more vegetables and less meat than in the cities.

Taylor observed also that in the rural areas clothing was in general good and adequate for all weather conditions, although again clothing was poorer in the arid areas and where there were sugar and cotton plantations. The real factors in the lower standard of life in rural Argentina compared with, say, the

United States or Canada were in housing and in the absence of motor cars and electricity for domestic and farming purposes. Anyone who has lived in the countryside among farmers in the Americas knows this as a fact of life. Electricity and the motor car are the agents for crossing a vast gulf from near-slavery and solitude to comparative freedom and independence.

The superiority of urban life, which drew people to the cities, consisted in the access to amenities like electricity, transport, education and entertainment. These had long been available to the upper class of landowners, professional men, managers and shopkeepers, and the wealthier landlords had taken the amenities of the city to the countryside for their own enjoyment. A working-class family budget published in 1940 by the information service of the Argentine Ministry of Foreign Affairs assumed that electric light, travel and newspapers were normally consumed in Buenos Aires by a family of wage workers with three children under 14 years of age. The 153 pesos per month in this budget, calculated on the basis of prices in Buenos Aires in May 1940, were spent largely on food and rent: 53 per cent for food, 22 per cent for rent and 14 per cent on clothing. This left little for what are now called 'cultural activities', and it allowed nothing for medical expenses or for savings and contributions to a retirement income.

If this budget was anything approximating to a description of reality, a great many workers in Buenos Aires were having a difficult time. Fully employed workers at that time worked from 140 to 190 hours a month. On 31 December 1939, for example, it was reported that 42 per cent of wage earners were working from 41 to 44 hours per week, 46 per cent between 45 and 48 hours, 8 per cent less than 40 hours and 2 per cent more than 48 hours a week. Some of these workers, for example laundresses, were earning as little as 2 pesos a day in the first half of 1938. On the other hand a typesetter was earning 1·66 pesos an hour for a 146-hour month, or about 262 pesos a month. He could afford to have three children, and might go to football games and take the family to the cinema, but the laundress certainly could not afford the luxury of children or being ill. Fortunately for her, the parks and the zoo were free.[36]

Wages tended to be best in the new industries such as the electrical industry or in skilled, organised industries such as the railways. Domestic service, general labouring in the meat-packing industry, working in textiles and tailoring were as ill-rewarded in Buenos Aires as elsewhere in the world. Wages in the countryside were very low, but generally they included board and lodging. A thresher-machinist earned about 1·60 pesos a day plus his keep in 1938.

It is difficult to estimate to what extent real income was increased by welfare provided by the state and other agencies not maintained by wage-earners themselves. The only notable free service provided by the public authorities in the 1930s was education, which included attention to the health of children and some provision of school meals. There were no unemployment insurance, public health service or old-age pensions. There was, however, a wide network of mutual societies and trade union pension schemes. These provided for the welfare of persons who were capable of sustaining membership in an organisation, had the means of contributing, and the continuity of employment necessary to provide pensions and other benefits. As everywhere the casual labourer, the ill-educated and the handicapped tended to be outside such autonomous systems financed by their members. About 4 per cent of the national budget in 1939 was spent on social welfare, but this represented grants to the National Low Cost Housing Board, and subsidies for charitable organisations and assistance to immigrants. The state, of course, maintained a system of pensions for civil and military personnel which accounted for nearly 6·8 per cent of public expenditure in 1939.

Education had long been free and compulsory. This was more adequately provided for in cities. The 12 per cent illiteracy rate among people over 14 years of age was largely due to poor rural schooling, and especially in the northern and north-western areas and in Patagonia. Poor facilities and indifference to education went together, and reinforced each other. In the cities and in the less sparsely inhabited rural areas, free schools provided education for 1,600,000 children between the ages of 6 and 14. Another 130,000 children were provided for in private schools of which a large percentage were Catholic. The German and English communities provided private schools which many Argentine children attended, but these accounted for comparatively few children.

The cost of primary education was borne by the national government and the provincial governments. In 1939, 12·5 per cent of the national expenditure went to provide for the National Council of Education which ran the 500 schools in the Federal Capital, and another 4,750 schools in the federal territories and in some of the provinces. The provinces supported another 5,600 schools.

The 12·5 per cent of the national budget spent on schools did not represent the whole sum spent on education by the national government. The Ministry of Justice and Public Instruction financed secondary education, normal schools for teachers and vocational and university education. About 83,000 young people were in public high schools, normal schools, commercial colleges and technical schools. Another 38,000 were in private secondary and vocational schools. About 30,000 were in universities. Altogether the Argentine community in 1939 spent more on its education than it did on its armed forces and about the same amount as on the servicing of the public debt.

The system of taxation in the 1930s was traditional and simple. In 1939 customs duties and port charges accounted for 38 per cent of total revenue and excise duties 16·8 per cent. Income tax constituted 10·9 per cent of the total, and inheritance taxes 1·8 per cent. A land tax amounted to 3·1 per cent. The income tax was levied at a rate of 5 per cent on all individuals and corporations subject to exemptions for dependents. Foreign corporations paid the same rates as Argentine corporations. Income exceeding 10,000 pesos per annum paid an additional 0·12 per cent on the excess, and incomes above 250,000 an additional 2 per cent. The transfer of income from the poor to the rich as a result of taxation was slight and did not equal the expenditure on education for the low income groups. The stability of prices and the low level of inflation prevented income transfers by the state through the use of the printing press and treasury bills. Smokers and drinkers of all classes supported the public revenues, and so did the owners of motor cars, although the taxes on petrol and oil were assigned 100 per cent to the National Highways Board for the building and maintenance of roads.

The Argentine budget in the 1930s fairly represented the values of the liberal oligarchy in the decade of infamy: to pay the debts of the state, to educate children, and to defend the nation. Unfortunately for the oligarchy, their creditors took advantage of them, their children repudiated them, and the armed forces attacked them.

Notes to this chapter are on pp 195–6

8

The response to war and change, 1940-1955

The Argentine economy of the 1930s has been depicted as one which had adjusted to the world catastrophe of depression with some skill and with better success measured in terms of comparative production and consumption than nations like the United States and Canada. This success had been conservative in the root sense of that word, for the governors of Argentina and the architects of their economic policies had preserved the basic structure of the economy as it had developed over three-quarters of a century, and had indeed strengthened that structure through salutary reforms. The rural sector was still the cornerstone of the economy, for its exports paid for the imports of the community and maintained the public credit. Dependence on foreign credit had been diminished, and so had reliance on foreign imports for certain consumer goods and raw materials, but it was still the case that Argentina relied for the effective functioning of its economy upon international trade in agricultural and pastoral products which paid not only for consumer goods but for the capital equipment, the semi-manufactures and the raw materials used by the growing industrial sector of the economy.

Even before the outbreak of World War II in September 1939 the Argentine economy was showing signs of renewed difficulties. 1937 had been a very successful year, but the poor crop of 1938, the uncertainties of world politics and the rising prices of Argentine imports shook confidence. Real wages began to fall and unemployment grew. The outbreak of war closed off some markets in Europe, and the fall of France and the Low Countries closed off still more. Britain's conversion to a total war effort under siege conditions threatened a principal market and diminished the supply of essential imports of industrial goods and coal. At this stage the Argentine government was obliged to do some fundamental thinking about its economic foreign policy as well as its international political alignments. Could Argentina any longer base its economic policy on the production of goods whose markets were in western Europe? Must Argentina not find alternative markets in the Americas? Must not Argentina so change the pattern of its productive activities that it would be less seriously affected by the instability, both economic and political, of the world overseas?

At this point the political arrangements on which the economy depended began to break down. In a history of the Argentine economy it is unnecessary to speculate on why this should have happened, but simply to note that it did happen and that the consequences for the economy of political incoherence became serious and have never ceased to be so since the break-up of the ruling coalition of the 1930s in the year 1941. In 1938 the Argentines had elected Roberto Ortiz to the office of President. He was the key man of Argentine politics inasmuch as he managed to maintain and promised further to develop a *modus vivendi* between the largest and most popular political party, the Radicals, which controlled the Congress, and the vested economic interests and the economic technicians who ran the Ministry of Finance, the Exchange Control Commission and the Banco Central. Unfortunately Ortiz was a diabetic, intellectually but not physically equal to the task he had to perform. In 1939 he began to go blind, and during 1940 his health deteriorated to the point where the Vice-President, Ramon Castillo, a narrow-minded, provincial conservative, was obliged to exercise the power of President.

In November 1940 the Minister of Finance, Federico Pinedo, obtained the approval of the Cabinet for a plan to meet the problems of the Argentine economy created by the war in Europe. The plan involved a scheme for mobilising the savings of the community through the sale of bonds bearing interest at 2 per cent. These bonds were to be used by banks to finance the purchase of crop surpluses, the building of low-cost housing and the expansion of industry. The plan took account of the facts of difficulties abroad, by dividing the world into three categories for the purposes of dealing in foreign exchange. The sterling area was recognised as one where Argentine exchange balances were growing and would continue to grow. These sterling balances were to be used to buy up British investments in Argentina then estimated at about £600,000,000, of which about 44 per cent were then earning no interest and profit and the rest returning about 2·4 per cent. The second area recognised was the transferable exchange area, principally the USA and Canada, where Argentina ran a trade deficit. Inasmuch as Argentina was purchasing military equipment in large amounts from the USA, it was planned to impose severe restrictions on imports of motor cars, electrical equipment, radio receivers and films from this area. The third area embraced Uruguay, Bolivia, Paraguay and Brazil where exchange was free and trade was to be encouraged and not impeded except by revenue tariffs. The Pinedo Plan was thus a programme to support the rural economy in the presence of the disruption of its markets, to create employment opportunities in construction and industry and to reduce the foreign share in the capital claims on the economy.

The plan required legislation by Congress. This the Congress refused to give on the grounds that the government was unyielding in the matter of disputed elections in the provinces of Mendoza and Santa Fe. The Vice-President refused to give way. Pinedo and his principal Cabinet colleague, the Minister of Foreign Affairs, Roca, then resigned. Instead of seeking the path of compromise the Vice-President reorganised his government, dug himself in and commenced ruling by decree. This marked the end of consistent, conservative management of the economy.

The new government of Vice-President Castillo did not have any new economic policies to put in the place of those of Dr Pinedo. In the last half of 1941 it began, however, to face up to the need to find new trade opportunities for Argentina now that Europe was sinking further into political chaos and disaster. In October the first commercial agreement with the United States since 1853 was negotiated. The object of the agreement was to open the channels of trade between Argentina and the United States, and to remove some of the obstacles which prevented Argentina from paying for American imports and investments of capital. The US agreed to reduce tariffs on 84 items constituting 93 per cent of Argentine exports to the northern republic. The tariff on big Argentine export items like linseed and canned meat was cut 50 per cent. The Argentines in return agreed to reduce tariffs on 127 items of import from the US constituting 30 per cent of American trade to Argentina. These included fish, fresh fruit, automobile parts, lumber and radio receivers. The Americans agreed that Argentina should not cut its tariffs until its currently depressed customs revenues reached the average of the customs revenues of the previous ten years. That the parties had some idea of a new orientation in Argentine economic foreign policy is suggested by the provision in the agreement for the establishment of a mixed commission to oversee the working of the new commercial policy of the two states.

The only thing very new in this agreement was the fact of the United States being a party. Its object was merely to improve trade, not to seek in the United States either capital or capital equipment for a revolutionary reorganisation of the Argentine economy. But the agreement had an importance beyond its stated terms inasmuch as the United States was in 1941 the only source of capital equipment upon which Argentina could rely for any further expansion of its economy and any strengthening of its infrastructure. For the previous thirty years or more the patterns of Argentine trade had been increasingly distorted by the Americans' determination to exclude some Argentine products absolutely from American markets and to put serious obstacles in the way of other products while at the same time increasing its sales in Argentina of motor vehicles, farm machinery, electrical equipment and films and simultaneously lending Argentina money. The agreement reduced, if it did not entirely remove, the agencies of distortion, and opened up new possibilities of development in Argentina, if the Argentines themselves wished to exploit them.

It was at this point that the Argentine government destroyed all possibility of exploiting the new arrangements with the United States for the purpose of economic development. The agreement had not yet been ratified when the United States was forced to declare war on Japan and her allies in Europe. At once the Americans sought to rally the American states to their side, and to mobilise the resources of the Americas for a vast war effort. The Mexicans and the Brazilians responded to the American bugle call but the Argentines did not. At the Pan-American conference in Rio de Janeiro in March 1942, Argentina refused to break relations with the Axis and declared for neutrality. In the circumstances of 1942, it is not surprising that the United States refused to have much more to do with Argentina economically. Brazil had already received the money and equipment to build a large steel plant and to improve the railway communications with its iron ore deposits. Mexico got steel plants and tin plate mills out of its lease-lend agreement with the United States. Argentina got nothing. For reasons which it is not here our business to analyse or to judge, the Argentine government refused to share in the stimulus to industrialisation which has always attended war, and to take advantage of the fact that for once the Americans were frightened enough to adopt a realistic policy about industrial development elsewhere than in the United States and on terms which considered the desire of less-developed countries for real control of what they were undertaking. Within a year the Argentines could keep their antiquated railways running only by burning linseed, maize and timber in the fire boxes of their steam locomotives, while the great waters of the Salto Grande flowed uselessly to the sea, as they still do. There were no hydro-electric power plants for Argentina, or diesel locomotives, or steel plants or tin plate mills, ie the things which Argentina needed to break out of its almost total dependence on agriculture and ranching as the means of keeping the economy healthy and the community rich. By the time the Argentine community woke up and General Perón began to talk expansively about industrial power and Argentina becoming a third force in world politics, the devastated communities of Europe and Asia were taxing to the limit the world's capacity to produce the capital equipment necessary for serious industrial growth.

The military *coup* of June 1943 did not seriously change the direction of Argentine policy in either the political or the economic sphere. One consequence of government by the generals and the colonels was, however, ominously harmful. While occupying the presidency Generals Ramirez and Farrell got rid of most of the economic technicians who had devised and managed the policies of the previous decade through the agency of the Ministry of Finance, the Exchange Control Commission, the commodity commissions and the Banco Central. It is not surprising, therefore, that the epoch of xenophobia and nationalism ushered in by the soldiers and brought to a peak of perfection by General Perón was barren of institutional innovation, and that the mechanisms of economic leadership and control devised by men like Pinedo, Duhau, de Tomaso and Prebisch were simply extended and operated badly to achieve ends for which they were never designed by men who appear to have had little real knowledge of what they were doing.

Given the determination to maintain a policy of neutrality, Argentina was frozen in the role of supplier of food and raw materials from 1939 to 1945. Ironically the military facts dictated that, neutral or not, Argentina supplied only one side: the United Nations. The facts of politics at the same time dictated that the United States continued to buy from Argentina, but for different reasons than in previous history, and continued to refuse to sell much to Argentina. Britain, on the other hand, was deprived by its war effort of supplying Argentina with coal and capital equipment and, under the terms of its Lease-Lend agreement with the United States, was debarred from supplying Argentina with tin plate, steel sheets and galvanised wire. Textile exports from Britain to Argentina were cut, and the export of cotton yarn was suspended early in 1942 and that of wool yarn in 1943. By the end of the war Britain was exporting to Argentina only a few bits and pieces of linen and rayon and industrial and pharmaceutical chemicals, glass, clay products, asbestos and whisky.

During the years of World War II Argentine exports contracted. Measured in 1950 prices, Argentina exported merchandise worth 7,397 million pesos during the years 1935–9. This fell to 5,963 million pesos during 1940–4. The decline was very uneven. The export of meat products increased and so did dairy produce. Wool maintained a level near the high levels created by stock-piling by the nations preparing for war in 1937–9. Agricultural exports fell heavily from 4,177 million pesos in 1935–9 to 1,890 million pesos in 1940–4.[1]

Far more serious for the economy was the decline in imports. Quantum indices of imports moved as follows (1935 = 100):

1939—99	1943—35
1940—84	1944—35
1941—65	1945—36
1942—54	

A study of the details of this decline reveals how serious this was in terms of the overall productive health of the economy. The quantity of food and tobacco imported did not fall as much as the general decline. Indeed tobacco imports rose absolutely, presumably so that people could take their minds off what was happening to imports of machinery, petroleum refining equipment and chemicals. The index of petroleum refining equipment was down to 20 in 1944; chemicals to 30; non-electrical machinery and vehicles to 8; electrical machinery to 12; metals to 19; solid fuel to 22, and so on.[2]

Exporting much more than they were importing, the Argentines were in effect lending heavily to the United Nations, neutrality notwithstanding. The government had agreed early in the war that Britain should pay for purchases in sterling deposited in the Bank of England and blocked there. The security for these loans was the British assets in Argentina. This was not stated in the agreement but it was a fact, for the Argentine government had power where the assets were. From 1942 onward the Argentine government began repatriating its sterling debt or liquidating it. By the end of 1944 approximately £75,000,000 of bonds had been repatriated or redeemed and in addition the Buenos Aires Waterworks Company and the Primitiva Gas Company had been expropriated, and the owners compensated. Even so, £60,000,000 stood to the credit of Argentina in blocked sterling balances in August 1944, and the Minister of Finance expressed the view that he ought to leave something in the account to finance the expected heavy purchase of equipment after the war was over.

In the case of purchases of Argentine produce by the United States, which for the first time exceeded by a large margin Argentine purchases of American goods, the Americans at first were happy to pay in gold, which the Argentines shipped to Buenos Aires to add to their reserves. In August 1944, however, the US Treasury prohibited further shipments of gold to Argentina. At that time, according to the Argentine Minister of Finance, Argentina owned 1,718 million pesos worth of gold in the United States.[3]

Nothing could more forcibly illustrate the ancient proposition that gold is not wealth than the situation of Argentina at the end of World War II. During the six years 1933–9 manufacturing output had increased 43 per cent; during the six years of war the increase was 23 per cent. The increase in the gross national product was more than cut in half compared with 1933–9. The net capital stock of machinery and equipment fell by 30 per cent.[4] Industrial transformation induced by war in countries like Canada, Australia, South Africa, Mexico and Brazil had not happened in Argentina. The growth of industry in Argentina during the war was concentrated in labour-intensive industries, and increased industrial production of textiles and similar consumer goods was achieved by using and over-using excess capacity. Meanwhile basic industries such as petroleum refining, transport and metal fabrication ran down. An illusion of prosperity was created by substantial wage increases, some given in response to the increased demand for labour and the cutting off of immigration and some in response to trade union pressure organised and encouraged by Colonel Perón in his desire for political power. The shift towards increasing the proportion of the gross national product spend on consumption rather than capital formation, which had been characteristic of the 1930s, continued. Given the then established emphasis on food, drink, tobacco and leisure as major components of popular wellbeing, an expansion of consumption was quite feasible within the limits of the then existing productive character of the economy. But popular expectations were beginning to change and the demonstration effects of events and patterns of life elsewhere were beginning to make their impact. Was the Argentine economy, so bountiful of beefsteaks, bread and wine, capable of meeting a demand for motor cars, refrigerators, more and better housing and political prestige in a world of arms and empires?

In spite of the running down of the productive capacity of the economy and the failure to broaden its base and strengthen its infrastructure during World War II, there were no inherent reasons why Argentina should not have embarked upon a course of steady and even spectacular economic growth once some sort of peace returned to the world. The potential for doing so was better than it had ever been in Argentine history. The Argentine community possessed large gold reserves and a large accumulation of promises to pay in the shape of blocked sterling. Labour supplies were better than they had ever been inasmuch as the native resources of labour in the north-western interior, in Paraguay, Bolivia and Chile, were being attracted into the Argentine labour market, making good the deficiency created by the cutting-off of immigration from Europe. Once hostilities ceased immigrants, too, began to flow into Argentina— 383,000 of them during 1946–50 compared with 3,000 during 1940–4.

If land, labour and capital are the basic components of production and hence of wealth, Argentina in 1946 was sufficiently possessed of these ingredients to maintain her position as one of the richest nations in the world. The problem was how to mix them, and how to administer the mixture. Up to this point in Argentine history the state had addressed itself to inducing capital investment and to increasing the supply of labour. The process of mixing and administering had been left largely, but not entirely, to private businessmen responding to the forces of the markets both domestic and international. The increased intervention of the state in the economy·during the 1930s was remedial rather than revolutionary. The statesmen and economic leaders of the 1930s had encouraged industry but they had not believed in 'industrialisation' as a road to salvation. They had taken control of exports and had taxed the rural interests for purposes they thought necessary, but they had not declared war on the export economy and the 'landed oligarchy'. They had reduced the share of foreign ownership of Argentine debts and enterprise in Argentina, but they had not denounced 'imperialism'. They had increased the share of state-owned productive enterprises in the economy, but they had not proclaimed themselves 'socialists'.

Juan Domingo Perón changed all this. In February 1946, he was elected President of the Republic. In his first message to the nation, Perón declared his intention to end the *laissez faire* system and to make the state the central agency in the direction and administration of the economy. All the tendencies of the 1930s in the direction of state ownership, control and direction were greatly accelerated. The Central Bank was nationalised. The railways were nationalised. The gas industry and a high proportion of central electricity generation were taken over by the state. The national merchant marine, begun during the war by the purchase of Danish and Italian vessels tied up in Argentine ports, was taken over completely by the state and expanded. Air transport was taken over. A steel industry was established as a mixed state and private enterprise. The Fabricas Militares, the industrial workshops of the armed forces, were expanded with the intention of establishing a state-owned aviation industry. The telephones and telecommunications were taken over. The role of the state agencies for marketing meat and cereals abroad was extended and a policy of price-fixing for producers and consumers was attempted. Insurance was nationalised. An all-embracing system of state pensions and health services was established. The fixing of rents and tenures of land was extended. Although the electricity generating capacity was already badly over-stretched, it was planned to develop an autonomous nuclear energy programme. By 1948 the state was in business in a big way.

A programme as grandiose as Perón's required a heavy investment of capital. His first estimate of its cost was US $1,500 million, not an impossible sum having regard to the size of the Argentine gold reserves and blocked sterling balances. Success, however, depended upon the careful and prudent expenditure of purchasing power upon the plant and equipment necessary to make good the long period of depreciation of machinery and plant which had been experienced from 1940 to 1945. In the case of the railways it was not just a matter of replacing old, worn-out rolling stock, but of scrapping the whole steam system, of re-equipment with diesel and/or electrical power and of decisions with regard to the relative importance to be attached to railways, roads and airlines in a national transport system.

Perón's rhetoric and his planning held out the promise of exciting new development. In fact the consequences of his real decisions differed little from the pattern of the 1930s. Popular consumption was further stimulated. The capital assets of the government were dissipated in paying off the owners of the enterprises which had been nationalised, and inasmuch as many of these were foreigners—British and French in the case of the railways, American and Belgian in the case of telecommunications—this ran down the reserves of foreign exchange. Some of the government's decisions were quite inexplicable in terms of commercial or financial logic. Bonds bearing interest at 3 per cent with distant maturities and quoted at 60–70 on stock exchanges and bourses were paid off at par. In no case did Perón's government follow normal capitalist practices in acquiring assets or initiate in any way the take-over bidders. The Argentine government could have secured control of foreign-owned railways, for example, by stock purchases for 10 per cent or less of what they finally paid in compensation to owners who bargained with them with the backing of their governments prepared to block Argentine assets held abroad. As it was, Perón and his ministers and advisers dissipated a substantial part of their assets buying up old iron, wires and pipes instead of purchasing new and up-to-date equipment capable of cheap and efficient operation and of extending the range and variety

F

of the productive apparatus of society. Thus, misled by unsound theories about imperialism unsupported by experience or observation, Perón and his advisers converted their socialist and nationalist ideals into a device by which large financial interests were able to unload enterprises they found it difficult to run upon even less qualified office-seekers and to deploy their generous compensation in greener pastures far away from Argentina.

The improvidence and errors of Perón were at first masked by a short-lived prosperity, bred, like much prosperity of the past, upon the widening of markets for Argentina's traditional exports and a sharp swing in the terms of trade in favour of Argentina. During 1946, 1947 and 1948 Argentine exports could buy more than at any time in history. Measured in terms of 1950 prices, Argentine exports had a price advantage of 20·3 per cent in 1946, 43·8 per cent in 1949, and 41·7 per cent in 1948.[5] This was a trading situation better even than that known in the golden years of prosperity before World War I. During these years, 1945–8, the gross national product increased by 29 per cent and greatly exceeded the increase of 16 per cent in population, including addition through immigration. Real wages per head of the economically active population rose from an index number of 127 to 162 between 1946 and 1948.[6]

These were the years when President Perón appeared to the people as a worker of miracles. A closer look at the wires which moved the miracle help to explain the collapse which came in 1949 and the renewed dependence on foreign capital which the President inaugurated in 1953.

At the heart of the failure of Perón and his advisers were decisions about investment. The conventional wisdom of Perón's critics, in so far as they ever discuss his economic policies, consists in asserting that he wrecked the economy by forcing or allowing a marked increase in wages, pensions and welfare services at the expense of capital accumulation and investment. There is very little in this analysis. Real wages rose much faster than productivity during the years 1941–9, but this increase in the real income of wage- and salary-earners was not unusual compared with other rich countries. What was different and serious in the Argentine case was the relatively static nature of the real gross domestic product. This rose from 110 in 1945–6 to 123 in 1947–9 while real wages were rising from 120 to 162.[7] Of the factors entering into this sluggish rise in the GDP the most important were the investment decisions of the government and the effect of their policies on the investment decisions of the private sector.

Looking first at the government investment, we find that the public authorities, which had been spending 21·3 per cent of the gross national product in the years 1935–9, were spending 29·4 per cent of the GNP in 1945–9. Considering that the state had taken over responsibility for investment in railways, the merchant marine, part of the electricity industry, telecommunications, gas distribution, waterworks, and harbour works previously owned privately, air transport and the nascent aviation industry, not to mention more fanciful and expensive projects like nuclear power, an increase in expenditure from 21·3 per cent to 29·4 per cent was an indication of inadequate investment. When, however, one considers that of the total expenditure of the public authorities only a fraction, of the order of 30 per cent, was spent on investment, one can see how meagre were the resources devoted to investment by the public sector. In 1935–9 the state had been investing 6·5 per cent of the GNP. In 1945–9 the percentage of GNP invested was 12·9, but of this a third, or 4·2 per cent of the GNP, was devoted to buying railways and gasworks, not to investment in additions to productive capital stock. In 1935–9 only 0·5 per cent of the GNP was devoted to such purposes. Thus we find that, for all its expenditure, amounting to nearly 30 per cent of the GNP, only 8·7 per cent was being invested in 1945–9.

And in what? During the years 1945–51 the average annual percentage of public investment on non-economic, non-productive equipment such as armaments and public buildings was 50–60 per cent. Some of these non-economic investments, such as sanitary works, made some contribution to productive life, but these accounted for about 4 per cent of all public investment compared with 29·3 per cent spent on armaments and 12·4 per cent on public buildings.[8]

Private investment, however, constituted still the largest proportion of total investment. It amounted to 15·7 per cent of the GNP. This represented a revival of private investment compared with 1940–4, but was still very much lower than the proportion of GNP invested before the depression and less than half the proportion invested before World War I. Foreign investment in Argentina almost ceased during 1945–9. It was down to 0·1 per cent of GNP compared with 1·5 per cent during the war years, 4·8 per cent in 1925–9, and 20·8 per cent in 1910–14.[9]

The direction of flow of this private investment was heavily towards manufacturing. Measured in terms of 1950 pesos, the capital in manufacturing increased from 17,146 millions of pesos to 28,287 million, whereas capital in rural production increased only 10 per cent from 31,067 millions to 34,068 millions. Capital in mineral production approximated to 40 per cent, and the capital in transport dropped about 8 per cent. These indications of the direction of the flow of investment overemphasise certain features of the flow during 1945–9. They are calculated on the state of capital stock in 1955. By this date Perón's government had changed its policies, and these must have influenced, if only marginally, the total of capital in, for example, the production of minerals.

In spite of the absence of figures specifically relating to the first phase of Perón's management of the economy, there can be no doubt about the general picture: an increase in investment in manufacturing, and a relatively low level of investment in agriculture and ranching. In this pattern something can be attributed to the management of bank credit. Shortly after nationalising the Banco Central and bringing it under close government control, the Bank was itself given the power to control the deposits and the lending policies and practices of all banks. Among the many purposes of this concentration of authority was the objective of diminishing the tenderness towards the rural interests which were alleged to characterise the conduct of bankers. The main factors, however, in the rapid growth of capital in industry and the relatively slow growth in the rural sector were the encouragement given to industry by tariffs, favourable consideration in the allocation of foreign exchange and a deliberate creation by the government of industrial interests. It is often alleged that Perón was concerned only with industrial workers. This was far from being the case. His government gave great help to industrialists, and, indeed, his insistence on high wages in industry improved labour supplies in industry at the expense of other activities.

If the government smiled on industry it frowned on agriculture and ranching. It did more than frown. The oligarchs of the decade of infamy and depression in the 1930s had taxed the rural sector through the agency of exchange control. Perón's government took over the marketing of rural produce through the state institution IAPI (Instituto Argentino de Promoción del Intercambio). This organisation bought up everything for export and sold it. When setting it up Perón made some very strong and encouraging statements about how he was going to end the bulk contracts for the sale of meat made during the war, and how he was going to introduce the rural interests to the delights and advantages of the rising prices of meat and cereals. In fact the terms of trade as between the products of the rural sector and what they could buy in international markets were extremely favourable, but IAPI saw to it that very little of this advantage accrued to the rural interests. For the first time in history the total number employed in the rural sector dropped, and so accelerated the long-term trend towards a smaller and smaller percentage of the economically active employed in agriculture and ranching.[10]

The measures taken by the government to win the support of the majority of those active in agriculture were designed to hamper rather than increase overall efficiency. The control of rents and tenures, although intended to help working farms, reduced the flexibility of the cereal-livestock economy, and fell between two stools. Rent control and the control of tenures did not give the farmers what many aspired to, ie independent possession of the land they worked, and on the other hand it reduced the possibility of both buying and renting land because ground landlords were reluctant to rent and so lose control of their land, and yet could not find buyers with capital sufficient both to buy and work land. There had long been a good case for a severe tax on land designed to hit the passive rentiers, and to benefit the active users of land—the working farmers and ranchers. But this was not Perón's solution. He was content to continue the system of taxing the rural interest in the way devised by the Concordancia of the 1930s. The difference consisted in doing so more severely and in a spirit of hostility.

During the years 1940–4 the total value of agricultural and pastoral production had been 13,401 million pesos at 1950 prices. In 1945–9 this dropped to 12,756 million. Simultaneously the proportion of agricultural and pastoral produce consumed in the domestic market began to grow. In the early 1930s, 50 per cent was consumed in Argentina and 50 per cent was exported. In 1944–9 the percentage consumed in Argentina had climbed above 70 per cent, and *per capita* consumption was about 13 per cent above that of 1935–9[11] but well below *per capita* consumption during the war years when the railway locomotives as well as the people were consuming cereals. The consumption of meat was up by nearly 10 per cent *per capita* compared with 1940–4.

The relatively static character of the rural economy and the increased internal consumption of the products of agriculture and ranching meant, of course, that less was available for export. From 1945 onward the favourable balance of Argentine trade on commodity account deteriorated steadily and heavily, as shown in Table 11.

TABLE 11

The balance of Argentine trade on commodity account,
1945–1951[12]

	Exports at 1950 prices (million pesos)	Imports at 1950 prices (million pesos)
1945	1,214·7	440·6
1946	1,408·2	861·0
1947	1,322·4	1,580·3
1948	1,153·6	1,629·3
1949	801·2	1,093·5
1950	1,144·9	964·2
1951	885·4	1,224·6

This was taking place in circumstances very favourable commercially to Argentina when the terms of trade were very advantageous. Furthermore it was taking place at a time when Argentine imports were no longer mainly consumer goods. In 1948 the proportion of fuel, raw material and goods used in industrial production to consumer goods imported was more than 2:1; in 1949 it was 4:1. The relative stagnation of agriculture and ranching and the increasing absorption of its products by the domestic market thus fixed a real limit to what could be imported for industrial use, because Argentina still relied as heavily as in the past upon the export of rural products to pay for imports. In 1948, 95 per cent of all Argentine exports were agricultural or livestock products, a percentage exactly the same as it had been in 1936 or 1926.

The harassment and exploitation of the rural sector and its consequent adverse effect on the Argentine balance of payments was not necessarily the cause of the crisis in the economy which developed in 1949. An expansive export trade in rural products and a good balance of payments would have widened the opportunities for industrial development by making easier the purchase of capital equipment and raw materials, but industrial expansion would still have been possible, had the investment decisions of the government paid sufficient attention to what may be described as the pituitary elements in the economy, ie electrical power production, transport, petroleum, and basic industrial materials like steel. The development of the pituitary elements was or had been taken into the public sector, and their development was therefore dependent upon the decisions of the public authorities and not upon the market.

Of the total investment made by the national government between 1945 and 1951, the average percentage on all forms of transport and all forms of energy production and telecommunications was only 41·2 per cent—and only 0·5 per cent on steel production—compared with 50·6 per cent invested in non-economic projects. When these total percentages are broken down, the neglect of the pituitary elements is revealed as very marked indeed: 4·3 per cent on fuel production and only 9·9 per cent on hydro and thermal electric plants and telecommunications. In the vital transport sector a higher percentage was spent on ocean and river transport than on railways, and more on roads than on either of these.[13]

A study of energy production made by the United Nations at the request of the Argentine government in 1959 revealed that energy production measured in kilograms of petroleum converted at a standard rate declined from 636kg per inhabitant in 1940–4 to 633 per inhabitant in 1945–9, and from 203kg per 1,000 pesos (at 1950 prices) of production in 1940–4 to 177kg per 1,000 pesos of production in 1945–9. In short, the demand for energy exceeded supply, and the shortages were affecting industry more than consumers generally. What a way to industrialise! The increase in the production of kwh per inhabitant had increased more than 30 per cent in the days of the incompetent, conservative oligarchy. Under the dynamic, forward-looking, planning and industrialising leadership of Perón, the growth had been cut in half, and this at a time when industries were being protected by tariffs, encouraged by subsidies and stimulated with rhetoric.

In the field of petroleum production the same insufficient growth could be observed. The state-owned oil company, YPF, which had tripled production between 1930 and 1945 in spite of shortages of machinery during the war years, increased production from 2,130,000 tons in 1940–4 to only 2,220,000 tons in 1945–9. This poor performance was not due to insufficient investment alone. In fact new investment produced the only redeeming feature of these years and the only really new development: the gas pipeline from Comodoro Rivadavia to Buenos Aires, opened in 1949. A major factor in the poor performance was the purging of the management of YPF for political reasons. Oil engineers and managers of world class were replaced by men who either did not know their jobs or were obliged to learn them at the expense of the enterprise.

The purchase of the railways from foreigners and the renaming of them after Argentine generals did not cause them to become more productive. The railways became a more manpower-intensive industry. Capital investment was ludicrously inadequate. The number of diesel electric locomotives increased from 33 in 1945 to 142 in 1950. The number of steam locomotives increased from 3,929 to 4,050. Of the steam locomotives, approximately 2,500 were more than 35 years old. Traffic increased from 83·3 million tons in 1941–5 to 91·2 million in 1946–50, but the number of people employed in the railways from 21,726 in 1943, to 23,206 in 1944, to 30,094 in 1949, and to 33,769 in 1951. Their wages rose by 65 per cent between 1943 and 1949. By 1953 Argentina led the world in numbers of railway personnel per 1,000 train kilometres, and in the percentage of expenditure of income on labour.

The public services, like the railways, became more manpower-intensive. The number of persons employed by the state grew from 448,000 in 1944 to 725,500 in 1950, or, put in another way, from 29,611 per million inhabitants to 42,208 per million inhabitants. Average income rose from 7,830 pesos (of 1950) per employee to 9,259 pesos (of 1950) in 1948 and then declined to 7,713 pesos (of 1950) in 1950. Total public expenditure rose from 8,957 million pesos (of 1950) in 1940–4 to 16,759 million pesos (of 1950) in 1945–9. Revenues from taxes and the sale of services rose from 7,187 million pesos (of 1950) in 1940–4 to 12,081 pesos (of 1950) in 1945–9. The gap between income and expenditure amounted to 3·8 per cent of the GNP in 1940–4, and to 8·2 per cent of the GNP in 1945–9.[14] How this gap was being financed was a critical point. In 1940 only 1·69 billion current pesos of public sector debt was in the hands of the Banco Central and the other public and private banks. By 1944 this had risen to 3·9 billion current pesos. By 1950 the amount was 17·52 billion current pesos.[15]

The idea of monetising the debts of the government, which the community had spontaneously rejected in the 1850s, now became acceptable to the ignorant and unthinking masses. The money supply began to grow, as shown in Table 12.

Quite naturally, inflation began to manifest itself. In 1944 the cost of living in Buenos Aires fell fractionally for the last time. It then started to rise as follows:

1945 + 19·7% of previous year
1946 + 17·7%

1947 + 13·5% of previous year
1948 + 13·1%
1949 + 31·1%
1950 + 25·5%

Overall wholesale prices followed the same course but not quite so markedly. Annual real hourly wages, which had risen 25·3 per cent in 1947 and 23·5 per cent in 1948, rose by only a modest 4·9 per cent in 1949 and fell 4·4 per cent in 1950.[17]

By the end of 1948 there were signs that the spree was coming to an end. By January 1949, it was over. On 19 January Miguel

TABLE 12

Billions of pesos at the end of each year[16]

	Currency bills in the hands of the public	Private demand deposits	Money supply	Bank deposits of low turnover
1945	2·64	3·83	6·47	4·69
1946	3·58	4·88	8·46	5·62
1947	4·77	5·48	10·25	6·24
1948	6·74	7·03	13·77	7·48
1949	9·07	8·51	17·58	9·42
1950	11·91	10·14	22·05	10·26

Miranda, the President of the National Economic Council, resigned. On 1 February the Banco Central stopped all applications for foreign exchange. The National Economic Council under a new president-chairman declared that government expenditure must be reduced, agricultural and pastoral production must be increased, exports must be increased, bank credits restricted and taxes increased. In June 1949, a bilateral trade agreement with Britain was negotiated. This was a carbon copy of the Roca-Runciman agreement of 1936 except in one important particular: it fixed the physical amount of meat Britain would buy and fixed its price, and it spelled out in amounts the quantities and value of steel, chemicals, textiles, machinery and whisky Argentina would buy from Britain. It fixed rules for the release of sterling and pesos for purchases and for conversion into other currencies. The United States protested, but in the end yielded to the Anglo-Argentine argument that the balance

of trade between Argentina and Britain was heavily favourable
to Argentina: that the American-Argentine balance was heavily
favourable to the US; and that in spite of a considerable improvement in US purchases of Argentine produce, the United
States still could not or would not buy sufficiently from
Argentina.

Perón's about-face in 1949 was not, however, a return to the
past. Nature itself did not co-operate with the Argentine
government. Serious crop failures impaired the volume of exports. In order to meet contractual obligations to supply meat
abroad, meatless days were ordered. Crop failures, however,
were what might be called casual factors. There were more
profound ones of a socio-economic and political kind.

The shortages of capital caused by the improvidence of the
past had to be made good. Furthermore, Argentina could not
go back to a total dependence on agriculture and ranching.
Agriculture and ranching were not manpower-intensive industries, and Argentine exports from the rural sector were not, and
never had been, the surpluses of a peasant economy capable of
sustaining and absorbing manpower at a low level of subsistence activity. The majority of the economically active population were wage and salaried workers employed in industry,
commerce, administration and the service trades. No amount
of improvement in agriculture and ranching could provide jobs
for the majority. The case for improving agriculture and ranching rested, as it still rests, upon the need to earn foreign exchange sufficient to pay for the means of industrial growth and
hence the means of employing people. To do this agriculture
and ranching have to be super-efficient, ie with the lowest
possible inputs in relation to outputs.

During the years between 1949 and his fall in 1955 President
Perón set about attempting to solve the problem of capital deficiency. In doing so he imposed a number of handicaps on
himself, all of them political. His populist style of political
leadership and the corrupt and bullying tactics of many of his
supporters created great uncertainty, fear and hostility among
the saving and investing classes. At the same time his anti-
imperialist nationalism set him against what he conceived to be

the agency of the international capitalist conspiracy, the International Monetary Fund. With this organisation he refused to have anything to do. In spite of these political difficulties which he generated for himself, President Perón was able, none the less, to find part at least of a solution to the deficiency of capital. After the hard fact of drought and crop failures in 1951, he succeeded in achieving a stabilisation which the International Monetary Fund was always recommending to its clients, and which its clients seldom effected. In 1950, 1951 and 1952 hourly real wages were cut by 4·4 per cent, 7 per cent and 11·3 per cent. By 1954 he achieved a surplus in the balance of payments. He cut the rise in public expenditure. This had risen from 8,957 millions of pesos (of 1950) in 1940–4 to 16,759 million in 1945–9. During 1950–4 expenditure rose only 1,250 million pesos. And he spent the public revenues more intelligently. Non-economic public investment was cut from 50·6 per cent of all public investment in 1945–51 to 27·4 per cent during 1952–5, and defence expenditure massively from 29·3 per cent to 9·7 per cent. Public investment in the production of fuel, electrical energy and telecommunications rose from 14·2 per cent to 24·4 per cent of investment expenditure in the same period, and transport investment from 27 per cent to 29 per cent. The production of electrical energy, which had amounted to 4,240kwh in 1945–9 was 6,770 million by 1955, and the percentage of hydro-electric energy was the best to date: 6·1 per cent. Crude petroleum production by YPF, which had increased only by a small fraction between 1944 and 1949, jumped from 2,220 million tons to 3,650 millions in 1955.

The overall picture of capital formation from 1950 to 1955 showed improvement. According to the calculations of the Banco Central, fixed capital formation was 114 billion pesos (at 1960 prices) in 1950. From this level fixed capital formation rose to 140 billion in 1951; 125 billion in 1952; 123 billion in 1953; 120 billion in 1954, and to 140 billion in 1955. This represents some sort of take-off. An inspection of the detail indicates that growth of fixed capital was greatest in machinery and transport equipment, although capital going into private construction was still comparatively high: 51 billion (at 1960 prices) in private construction in 1950 compared with 27 billion in machinery and equipment; but in 1955 43 billion in machinery and equipment compared with 48 billion in private construction.

During the years 1951 to 1955 signs of serious qualitative change in the industrial sector were beginning to emerge. In 1951 motor vehicles began to be manufactured and not just assembled in Argentina. In that year 108 vans and lorries were produced. In 1953 five motor cars were produced. By 1955, 6,391 vehicles were produced of which 211 were motor cars. In 1954, the Argentine government entered into an agreement with H. J. Kaiser, the American entrepreneur, to establish a joint enterprise for the production of motor vehicles. The government and Kaiser were jointly to own 51 per cent of the shares, and the rest were sold to private Argentine capitalists. From the Argentine government's point of view this represented the liquidation of a romantically conceived plan to found an aviation industry. Under the agreement they merged Industrias Aeronauticas Mecánicos del Estado with Industrias Kaiser Argentina, and thus converted the aviation plants in Córdoba to the production of motor cars.

An indicator of the maturity and sophistication of an economy is its consumption of steel per head of population. In 1940–4 this was 20 kilograms *per capita*, or less than one-seventh of the consumption *per capita* in the years 1905–14. During the first phase of Perón's industrialisation the consumption of steel *per capita* rose to 62kg, a figure still below the level of 1935–9. In 1950–2 the level of consumption was down almost to the 1940–4 level, but recovered sufficiently with renewed investment to bring the average consumption in 1950–4 to 54kg *per capita*. In 1955 the consumption rose to 86kg, still short of consumption in 1925–9, or before World War I, but the best for twenty-five years.[18] Even so, it was a level of consumption less than one-third that of Australia and one-quarter that of Canada.

An important feature of Perón's economic about-face during the years 1949–55 was abandonment of nationalist policies of hostility to foreign capital. Until 1949 his policy had been to diminish or eliminate foreign participation in the Argentine economy mitigated only by a policy of encouraging foreign firms to establish plants in Argentina. In November 1948, his government reported with satisfaction that it had introduced £12,500,000 of foreign capital and 25,000 foreign industrial workers and managers, and that this had resulted in the establishment of 31 metallurgical plants, 27 construction firms, 12 textile factories and 5 chemical plants. Obviously these were on average small enterprises. In 1953, however, his government signed an agreement with Standard Oil of California giving to this company exploration, drilling, refining and distribution rights in Argentina. Foreign motor manufacturers began to enter Argentina. By the time of his fall in 1955 Perón had established a pattern of further industrialisation which involved a large-scale participation of multi-national corporations in manufacturing and the production of industrial raw materials and intermediate goods. This was a development which did little to promote the growth of a native class of industrial capitalists as distinct from managers and workers. In fact by 1955 the key growth points in the Argentine economy were less in Argentine hands then they had been in the days of the oligarchy. This result had been achieved behind a smoke-screen of rhetoric about the International Monetary Fund and the evils of neo-imperialism.

The name of Perón is inevitably associated with the growth of trade unions. Before Perón took over the secretariat of labour and converted it into a ministry in 1943, there were less than half a million members in the trade unions of Argentina: 472,828 according to a report in 1941.[19] At an extraordinary congress of the Confederación General de Trabajadores in 1950 the membership was reported to be four million. This figure meant that approximately two-thirds of the economically active population were members of trade unions. This growth had been accompanied by a large improvement in the real income of wage and salaried workers and a vast extension of social benefits such as pensions and health services. What effect the expansion of trade unions had on production is not so evident. In industries like transport productivity fell, although this cannot be attributed to the fact of trade unions. The railways in particular had long been staffed by well-organised workers. In the labour-intensive building trades, however, there seems to have been a connection between the rapid growth of unions and union rule-making and the severe decline in output per man-hour. In a report written in 1955 Raúl Prebisch, the economist, found that the man-hours required per square metre of construction had nearly doubled between 1939 and 1955, and another study of overall productivity in the construction industry indicated an approximate decline of 25 per cent at a time when the overall productivity had been improving by approximately 10 per cent.[20] A trend towards declining productivity per employee in the construction industry was particularly serious because construction accounted for a large, perhaps unduly large, share of capital investment.

There were, however, some bright spots in the economy which must be noticed. From 1943 onward there developed in the urban surface transport business in Greater Buenos Aires and in other Argentine cities a system of worker-owner organisations which resulted in good incomes for the workers and abundant service for the public. Everywhere *colectivos* took the place of tram companies. These were motor buses owned in many instances, but not all, by their drivers and other workers in the industry. That a great city like the Federal Capital of Argentina and its vast surrounding suburbs could be supplied with a cheap and frequent service of autobuses without the alleged benefits of central organisation, management and investment represented a new departure in entrepreneurial initiative, and a contradiction of conventional economic wisdom. The *colectivos* are motor buses capable of carrying 25–30 passengers seated and in maximum use nearly as many passengers standing. They are generally owned by a syndicate of workers who hold a franchise to run over routes designated by the municipal authorities. Fares and schedules are fixed by the authorities, and some inspection of service is maintained. The rest of the operation, including the raising of capital, maintenance of the equipment, keeping of accounts, the driving of the buses and the collection of the fares, is left to the worker-owners, who constitute a modern version of a medieval guild.

The system is flexible, and it does not preclude companies of capitalists owning equipment and hiring workers, but the main character of the system is maintained by the predominance of owner-operators. The *colectivo* system represents a great pool of organisational experience and talent as well as capacity for hard work which has the potential of replacing the railways and providing a comprehensive service of transport both of people and goods while at the same time solving the problem of relations between capital and labour.

The effect of more all-embracing organisations of wage workers on immigration and labour supply was ambiguous. In the United States, Canada and Australia the labour movement had succeeded in checking the influx of immigrants. In Argentina this had not happened, and during Perón's first period of office immigration, though below the massive figures of the early twentieth century, had accounted for a net increase of population of 383,000. After 1950 immigration fell off, partly owing to economic conditions in Argentina and their comparative improvement in Europe and partly owing to the imposition of selective controls. Between 1951 and 1955 net immigration declined to 201,000. This was, however, offset by an influx, often illegal, of an indeterminate number of Chileans, Bolivians, Peruvians and Uruguayans, many of whom flowed in to fill the gaps in service employments left by those moving into factory industry.

As a politician Perón laid much emphasis on the development of the Argentine interior, and the reversal of the long historical trend towards concentration of activity in the Litoral. It cannot be said, however, that much was achieved. The census of 1947 showed 29·7 per cent of the population concentrated in Greater Buenos Aires. The census of 1960 showed 6,763,000 living in Greater Buenos Aires: a percentage of 33 per cent. No shift was so marked elsewhere, and some provinces like La Pampa and Santiago del Estero actually suffered an absolute decline in population. Some of the Andean provinces like Salta, Jujuy and Mendoza grew, and their capital cities showed evidence of progress, but this did not amount in any way to a transformation. Córdoba, regarded as a showpiece of industrial development outside the Litoral, grew, but not as fast as Buenos Aires. In 1947, 9·3 per cent of the population of Argentina lived in the province of Córdoba. By 1960 this percentage had declined to 8·8 per cent.

Notes to this chapter are on p 197

9

Industrialisation,
1955-1971

Whatever measure of success President Perón may have had during the years 1951–5 in his endeavours to correct the faults and make good the economic waste of his first term in office, he failed to achieve that minimum degree of social and political agreement necessary for the working of any social system. He was overthrown by a *golpe de estado* in September 1955. Between then and 1971 no less than eight men held the office of President of the Argentine Republic: two as the result of elections and six of *golpes* by the armed forces. Thus, to the uncertainties of nature and market forces there were added the uncertainties of politics with which the economically active population had to contend. Political uncertainty aggravated economic uncertainty. The politicians, whether they liked it or not, were obliged to direct the economy and were advised in this by professional economists whose displays of technical expertise could not conceal their disagreements both about diagnoses and prescriptions. Like their masters, none of the economists remained sufficiently long in office to see a policy through, with the consequence that, although there was always a policy being tried, none had time to work, if work it would.

Given the instability of the socio-political environment, the development of the Argentine economy since the crisis of 1949–51 represents a triumph of some kind. During the last two decades the Argentine economy has grown and matured in terms of producing for itself the muscle and sinew of an industrial society in the shape of steel, petroleum derivatives, chemicals and engineering products with a supporting infrastructure of electrical energy. By 1970 those features of sophisticated industrialisation so conspicuously lacking in 1950 were conspicuously present.

In 1955 Argentina was producing approximately 200,000 tons of steel a year, was importing 84 per cent of its annual consumption and was consuming only 86 kilogrammes per head of population. Production did not improve noticeably until 1960. Thereafter it rose from 277,000 tons that year to 1,250,000 tons in 1964, 1,327,600 tons in 1967 and 1,775,000 tons in 1970.[1]

The petroleum industry was, of course, much better established by 1955, and was producing 5,000,000 cubic metres of crude oil a year at that time. Ten years later Argentina was producing 15,500,000 m^3 a year, and in 1971 27,000,000 m^3. Argentina is one of the world's minor but important producers. If production was only one-thirtieth of that of the USA, one-tenth of that of Venezuela and one-third of that of Canada in 1965, Argentina was none the less the fourth largest producer in the Americas, and produced more than any European country except the USSR. In terms of processed petroleum, the production of motor fuel grew from 3,000,000 m^3 in 1961 to 5,300,000 m^3 in 1970, and the production of diesel oil increased 80 per cent during the same period.[2]

During the 1950s and 1960s the production of motor vehicles became firmly established. In 1951, 108 vehicles were produced and by 1955 this figure was 6,391. In 1960, 89,338 vehicles were produced; in 1965, 194,536 vehicles, and in 1969, 218,590. In 1968 there was one motor vehicle for every 12 people in Argentina compared with one for every 31·3 in Brazil, one for every 550 in Haiti, one for every 2 people in the United States and one for every 4·3 people in Britain.[3]

In 1955 Argentina was generating 6,000 million kilowatt hours of electricity. By 1970 this figure had risen more than 2½ times to 16,891 million kwh.[4] The figures for the period 1970 somewhat under-represent the growth because the Argentine statistics since the late 1960s do not include electric power generated privately by industries for their own use.

Measured in terms of 1960 prices the gross internal product

at factor cost grew from 688,589 million pesos in 1950 to 798,133 millions in 1955 to 1,335,868 millions in 1969. During the 1950s and 1960s the non-Argentine contribution to the gross national income remained very small. During President Perón's second term in office the proportion was as little as 0·002 per cent and never above 0·05 per cent, but even in 1969 when the government was devoted to international economic co-operation the foreign contribution to the Argentine gross national income was less than 1 per cent.[5]

The growth of production during the 1950s and 1960s was uneven, as one might expect in any process of transformation. Put in general terms, the extraction of minerals, the manufacturing of metal products and the production of energy grew much more rapidly than agriculture and ranching. A simple table of index numbers based on physical volume (Table 13) suggests the pattern.

TABLE 13
Index numbers of growth of production, 1950–1969
(*1960 = 100*)

	Total production	Agriculture etc	Total industrial products	Extraction of minerals	Manufacture of machinery, etc
1950	74·4	81·1	66·8	36·8	37·7
1951	77·3	86·5	68·6	42·7	39·0
1952	73·4	73·8	67·3	45·4	41·1
1953	77·4	96·9	66·9	48·7	42·3
1954	80·5	96·4	72·2	51·6	46·6
1955	86·3	100·5	81·1	53·6	56·8
1956	88·7	95·8	86·7	54·9	62·9
1957	93·2	95·2	93·5	58·7	75·7
1958	99·1	99·5	101·3	62·9	83·5
1959	92·6	98·6	90·9	72·6	75·7
1960	100·0	100·0	100·0	100·0	100·0
1961	107·1	99·2	110·0	130·8	113·9
1962	105·3	103·4	103·9	147·3	105·7
1963	102·8	105·5	99·7	146·8	96·0
1964	113·5	112·7	118·4	149·5	124·8
1965	123·9	119·3	134·8	155·1	145·2
1966	124·8	114·6	136·0	163·7	143·6
1967	127·9	119·7	137·9	183·5	144·6
1968	133·8	114·7	147·4	206·2	153·8
1969	144·4	119·8	163·7	216·5	181·8

This record of increase and transformation is not, however, viewed with satisfaction by the Argentine community. When the Argentines compare the income per head generated by the development of the 1950s and 1960s with that of other similar communities, they express disappointment. The *per capita* income of Argentina increased from US $407 per head in 1950 to $703 in 1969, but the *per capita* increase in Australia was from $604 to $1,945 during the same period.[6] In terms of their expectations—even carefully planned ones—production has fallen short. The national plan of 1965, for example, projected near self-sufficiency in steel by 1969, and set the production target for that year at 4,000,000 tons. Actual production that year was 1,700,000 tons. A long-run growth rate since 1950 under 3 per cent pa has been a source of dissatisfaction in the presence of persistent growth rates of more than 6–7 per cent pa and higher in Mexico and Brazil. Not only has the growth rate been low. It has been very uneven. During four out of twenty years the volume of production has fallen compared with the previous year; during four years the gross national income at constant prices has fallen similarly; and during five out of twenty years the gross internal product at market prices has fallen. According to the statistics kept between 1963 and 1971, unemployment was never less than 4·7 per cent and was as high as 8·8 per cent in 1963, 7·4 per cent in 1964 and 6·8 per cent in 1967.[7] In 1964 unemployment was 9 per cent in some areas.[8] Between 1961 and 1965 unused capacity in manufacturing generally never fell below 30 per cent, and no industries operated above 95 per cent capacity.[9] Nothing in the experience since 1965 suggests a substantial alteration in this tendency towards a high proportion of unused capacity, some of it clearly manifest in idle men and machines and under-utilised land and some concealed in over-manned enterprises and institutions such as the railways and the state bureaucracies.

Inflation measured in terms of overall wholesale price increases has been a persistent phenomenon. In the last two years of the Perón regime the wholesale price increases of the years 1948–52 were brought under control and in 1954 had been reduced to 3·2 per cent. Since 1955 the percentage increase in overall wholesale prices during a year over the previous year has fallen below 10 per cent on only two occasions: in 1961 and 1968. In 1959 the increase was 133·5 per cent, and the average annual increase between 1955 and 1971 has approached 30 per cent. Inflation has seriously disturbed the match between savings and investment,[10] and the capital market which was beginning to develop in Buenos Aires in the late 1930s has virtually disappeared. The expectations of all participants in the economic system have been seriously disorganised, and this has bred deep social and political antagonisms. The search for security by individuals has led to heavy investment in real property and to the flight of capital and skilled personnel abroad. The vacuum thus created has presented opportunities for large multi-national corporations with the power to negotiate with governments and to plant themselves and their expert personnel in Argentina. This has been conspicuously so in the case of the manufacture of motor vehicles and to a lesser extent in chemicals and the electrical and electronic industries.

The conscious determination to transform Argentina into a mature industrial society and the activity of doing so have generated a number of economic problems which help to explain the poor performance so worrying to Argentines. In certain key areas of industrial activity, for example, the size of the market and the determination to supply it through exclusively Argentine effort have inevitably involved high costs in relation to the output necessary to meet the demands of the Argentine market. In 1969 the prices of motor cars manufactured in Argentina were from 185 per cent to 266 per cent above the level of the same motor cars manufactured by parent firms in the United States, Italy and France. This was the situation in 1969 in spite of the fact that there had been a decline in the selling price of motor vehicles in Argentina varying from 25 per cent to 32 per cent during the years 1960–9.[11] In 1969 the Association of Motor Manufacturers invited a team of economists to investigate these high costs. They reported that the biggest single factor in the high prices of motor cars manufactured in Argentina compared with those manufactured in North America and Europe is the small scale of the manufacturing operation in Argentina and the consequent high overhead costs. Other big factors are tariffs on imported material and the requirement imposed by the state that they use locally produced raw materials. These economists found that nothing could be attributed to Argentine wage rates and welfare payments, and very little to profits on manufacture and to Argentine levels of taxation.[12]

Even without the benefit of analyses of costs similar to that of the motor industry there are strong reasons for believing that many, if not all, of the newer industries established during and since World War II have high costs of operation. It is evident, for example, that Argentine industry has not become a big factor in the international market for industrial products in the way that Japanese industry has. It has not done so even in neighbouring countries in South America. Until 1967 Argentine fiscal ingenuity was devoted to keeping the products of foreign industry out of Argentina, and the presumption is that Argentine manufacturers could not stand foreign competition. Since 1967 tariffs have begun to come down from their astronomical heights in the hope that Argentine manufacturers may not only be able to meet competition at home but begin to export abroad. There have been increases in 'non-traditional exports', ie the products of new industries not processing food or rural products, but in 1969 the proportion of these exports was still only 15 per cent compared with the 85 per cent made up of cereals, meat, leather, wool, etc. It is a fair supposition that Argentina is not a great exporter of electrical generators for the same reason that it is not a great exporter of motor vehicles.

If the industrialisation of Argentina were possible as a nationally autonomous enterprise in the way that it tended to be in the United States during the nineteenth century and the first half of the twentieth, the effect of high costs at one stage of the process would not affect the ongoing process and might lead to the emergence of falling costs, as indeed there were signs of in the Argentine motor vehicle industry in the late 1960s. Unfortunately Argentina cannot industrialise independently of other communities. Industrialisation has changed the pattern of connections with other communities but it has not diminished them. Industrialisation has diminished the demand for consumer goods such as textiles, refrigerators, whisky, furniture, etc, but it has greatly increased the demand for fuel, raw and semi-manufactured materials and tools and machines. Between 1935 and 1961 imports of tobacco, for example, fell by 95 per cent and imports of metallic minerals multiplied by a factor of 40; vehicles and machinery by a factor of 4·7 and electrical machinery imports doubled.[13]

These imports, indispensable to the industrialising process, have had to be paid for, and the only means of paying for them has been to export the products of agriculture and ranching. Until 1967 there was only one occasion—during World War II —when agropecuarian products paid less than 90–95 per cent of the foreign bills of the Argentine Republic, and today the proportion is still well above 80 per cent. The rural sector has always been, and still is, the key sector in the Argentine economy, whether the Argentines were engaged in the simple-minded activity of consuming as much as possible or in the more sophisticated game of industrialising themselves. But industrialising has created a number of problems—some inevitably economic and some man-made and political—for the rural sector. In the first place the outputs of industry constitute a substantial part of the inputs of agriculture and ranching, and the outputs of industry are costly. Industrial inputs in agriculture and ranching have been increasing all over the world, and especially in North America, Europe, the Far East and Oceania where Argentina's markets and competitors are. In Argentina this has been happening, too, but at high cost. A 50hp tractor in 1965 actually cost more in terms of the amount of cereals needed to buy it than it did in 1947.[14] From 1940 onward the terms of trade between the rural sector and the industrial sector in Argentina have been continuously and sometimes disastrously adverse, measured in terms of general prices or implicit prices or in terms of selected commodities consumed by the rural sector.[15] Since 1966 there has been some evidence, however, of a fall in the relative prices of industrial inputs into agriculture and ranching such as chemical fertilisers, pesticides and tractors.

Another important circumstance affecting agriculture and ranching has been the fact that the outputs of the rural sector are a major element in the real wages of the industrial workers. Food constitutes approximately 30 per cent of the workers' expenditure in Buenos Aires and is not far short of this proportion in other industrial centres such as Córdoba. If goods manufactured out of rural products such as textiles, leather goods, tobacco and alcoholic beverages are included in the workers' budgets, the proportion is well over 50 per cent.[16] If the price of rural products rises as a result of increased demand abroad, drought in Argentina or alteration in exchange rates, the effect on real wages is immediately felt and the response quick. The wage workers are organised and urbanised. The day is long past when adverse circumstances forced them to return to Spain and Italy or to seek employment at subsistence rates in the countryside. The pressure of the workers both industrially and politically is immense. Perón resisted workers' pressure in the interests of stabilisation and getting the economy moving in a new direction during 1953–5, and Onganía did so during 1967–9, but no government has ever been strong enough to maintain pricing policies for the rural sector at levels necessary to maintain an adequate flow of the high-cost industrial inputs which the rural sector requires if it is to avoid technological stagnation.

While agricultural and pastoral output has been rising in comparable countries like Australia, Canada and the United States and in western Europe, the rural economy of Argentina has tended to resemble that of the USSR in terms of stagnant productivity. Productivity in the countryside has increased, but not as fast as population nor nearly as fast as the economic demands made upon it. In 1947 the cattle population was 258 per cent of human population. In 1968 it was 218 per cent. The production of meat fell from 127 kilograms *per capita* to 104·9 *per capita*. On the agricultural side, oil seeds and forage crops dropped 1·79 tons *per capita* in 1939 to 1·08 tons in 1968, and total agricultural production from 2·40 tons *per capita* in 1947 to 1·88 tons in 1968. Only in fruits and vegetables was there evidence of a slight growth in terms of output per head of population.[17]

The static character of the agricultural sector can best be described in terms of total production and total area utilised. The area sown to wheat was 9,219,000 hectares in 1929. This figure has never been exceeded, and during the past twenty years the area sown to wheat has been on average 20 per cent less than in 1929. In 1939 the Argentine wheat crop was 10,100,000 metric tons: a record. It has approached this total only once since then, in 1965. In only six years out of the period 1950–70 did wheat production exceed 7,000,000 metric tons. Given the areas sown, the Argentine production per hectare has improved slightly more than the USSR, Australia and Canada, but less than the United States and very much less than France, England and Mexico. The three-year average of 1961–3 was 21 per cent better than the three years 1947–9 in terms of production of wheat per hectare.[18] In the case of other cereals the picture is the same, except in the case of linseed which has experienced a large decline in area sown and total production and a fractional decline in productivity per hectare, and in the cases of sunflowers and sorghum where there has been great growth. The overall state of agriculture during the decades 1950–70 has been, thus, one of sluggishness, of some change of emphasis, of some improvement of production per person employed, and of some improvement in land utilisation, but there has been no growth sufficient to meet expanding internal demand and to sustain the heavy weight upon the balance of payments on commodity account occasioned by the demands of industry in international markets for materials and machinery and for which Argentine industries cannot themselves pay.

Apart from the factors of high-cost industrial inputs into agriculture and ranching and the pressure exerted on governments to keep down the prices of rural outputs, there has been an atmosphere of hostility in the community to the landed interest on account of their wealth and supposed political and social power. Since the 1930s taxes have been levied on exports directly and through the agency of exchange controls. Even when it has been decided by the political authorities to encourage the rural sector in the interest of improving the balance of payments by revaluing the peso the government has felt obliged to prevent 'windfalls' to the agricultural and ranching interests. In 1967, for example, the Minister of Economy, Dr Adelberto Krieger Vasena, revalued the peso and brought down its value in terms of the more stable currencies of Europe and the United States, but he simultaneously imposed 25 per cent duties on the exports of cereals, meat and oil grains, thus neutralising the advantage of devaluation to agriculture and ranching.

In response to the agitation of tenant farmers and in an effort to protect them the governments since the 1930s have controlled land rents. The institutionalisation and extension of controls, originally intended to save working farmers from bankruptcy caused by rapidly falling cereal prices in the early 1930s, has had the effect of destroying the flexibility of land use which was once one of the strengths of Argentine rural enterprise. Landowners have been reluctant to rent, and renters to end their tenancies and seek better terms for better opportunities. The result has been a great decline in tenancies. The number of tenancies in the pampean zone declined from approximately 120,000 to 50,000 between 1947 and 1960.[19] The result has not been the creation of a substantial class of medium-size rural landowners. The worst of both worlds has been achieved: a growth of uneconomic minifundia worked at subsistence levels; and latifundia worked only up to the level that the proprietors consider desirable in the light of their treatment by the public authorities and the cost of inputs in relation to outputs. Furthermore, investment in land as a hedge against inflation has pushed up land values without adding to the number of working farmers and ranchers professionally interested in and capable of producing. The inheritance laws requiring the division of properties equally among heirs has led to the formation of family land-holding corporations, thus reinforcing the tendency to latifundia. One study made in the early 1960s indicated that 3 per cent of all land was exploited in areas too small for efficient operation; another 20 per cent in tenancies of an economic size but subject to such uncertainty of prospects that efficiency of use was impaired; and that 25 per cent of land in latifundia was not fully exploited. In 1967 legislation to end rent controls was enacted, which obliged tenants to buy and landlords to sell to tenants, or to re-negotiate tenancies in accordance with market criteria. This has had some effect, but the prospect of creating an active land market in which working farmers predominated such as existed before the 1930s depended upon ending inflation and allowing farmers and ranchers to respond freely to the market opportunities created by growth in demand at home and abroad. In 1967 an attempt was made to levy a new land tax but this effort was so feeble that it provided little or no incentive on the part of owners to increase production in order to diminish the proportionate burden of taxation.

The high cost of industrialisation on the basis of a home market, small in relationship to the overhead costs of industry, is inevitable, at least in the developmental stage. This high cost of industrialisation may be described as an unavoidable economic phenomenon which is a natural obstacle to an exact match between the growth of industrial output and the growth of distributed real income. This natural economic fact has, however, been reinforced by political factors of a cost-increasing and real-income-decreasing character. The demand for income opportunities has been met only in part by the creation of real economic opportunities to produce wealth. In part it has been met by the creation of unproductive jobs and by the development of rackets. This is not a specifically Argentine or Latin American phenomenon but it exists in Argentina on a sufficient scale to be noticed. The state bureaucracy performs necessary functions which have legitimate costs chargeable to economic activity, but the bureaucracy is manpower-intensive and has grown faster than population. Between 1967 and 1970 salaries and pension contributions of the national government rose from 1,913 million pesos to 3,153 million pesos.[20] In spite of these increases the real incomes of civil servants have not kept pace with the cost of living. The tendency of the state-owned railways towards manpower-intensive operations has already been noticed, and, in spite of efforts at correction in the late 1960s, the problem is still there. The armed forces are likewise a non-productive income-distribution system. Pay and allowances account for a major part of defence expenditure, and to be an officer in the armed forces is a way of securing an income for life. It should be remarked, however, that, prominent as the armed forces are in Argentine political life, their costs are not a drain on the economic resources of society comparable with the drain in states like the USA, the USSR, and the United Kingdom. The Argentine armed forces are not particularly well equipped by the standards of the great powers and their imitators, and are not even a very good secondary stimulus to industry.

Outside the public sector rackets have taken their toll and put up costs. Until the drastic purge and reorganisation of the docks in 1967–8, the control exercised by the dockers' unions increased costs, reduced efficiency and limited job opportunities to the point where insurance and shipping companies made a surcharge on all shipments to Argentine ports to cover thefts, delays and rake-offs. A measure of the extent of racketeering and its costs can be judged by the fact that firm control and reorganisation in 1967 reduced the turn-around time of grain ships in Argentine ports from 12·5 to 2·1 days. This was achieved without reducing legally established wage rates or legally established rates for handling various types of cargo.

The overthrow of President Perón in 1955 produced a euphoric disposition to nostalgia: a widespread belief that Argentina could return to the 'good old days' of intimate and free economic and financial relations abroad and open democracy at home. Unfortunately the world of *laissez faire* had been dead for twenty-five years. The world abroad had changed, and in Argentina a vast web of interests and pressure groups had developed whose claims and importunities could not be set aside by a *camarilla* of revolutionary officers, better at expressing public complaints than at finding solutions. None the less, the disposition towards economic internationalism was there. It was expressed concretely in the decision to join the International Monetary Fund and to seek to live by its rules. IAPI, the state trading monopoly, was liquidated. The multiple exchange rates, which Perón had maintained with an upper limit of 14 to the US dollar (when its black market price was 30 to the dollar), were ended and the peso was devalued. Quantitative restrictions on imports were progressively abolished, and price controls were lifted. This sounded like a revolutionary liberal programme, but it was, in fact, a series of half-measures designed to please everyone and consequently unable to achieve the objective of an alternative economic policy. The devaluation to 18 pesos to the dollar still left the peso heavily overvalued. The import restrictions were replaced by import surcharges. The effects of freeing the market in agricultural products were attenuated by a policy of retentions, or export taxes. Price controls were lifted, but not on beef.

Between 1956 and 1959 there was some economic growth, but nothing to suggest that the economy was being managed dramatically better than Perón had done. In 1959 production fell compared with 1958. In 1959 all import restrictions and price controls were eliminated, and the peso was allowed to float. It at once floated down to 83 to the US dollar, which was close to the black or parallel market rate. Export retentions and import surcharges were retained, but a system of exemptions in favour of industrial requirements was instituted. As a result of the effective devaluation of the peso and the decision of President Frondizi to allow foreign oil companies more freedom in Argentina, there was an inflow of foreign capital. Economic growth followed, but once again compromise prejudiced policy. The free floating peso was fixed at 83 to the dollar, just at the time when the agricultural and ranching interests were beginning to invest and increase production. Then a bad crop year followed in 1961. The economy was once more in crisis, and the crisis was intensified by increased foreign debt obligations and outflows of capital.

In 1962 President Frondizi was overthrown and a further step was taken towards *laissez faire*. A freely fluctuating exchange rate was introduced and the system of retentions on exports was abandoned. In 1963 a democratically elected government was installed. As a political gesture, President Illia cancelled the oil contracts with foreign companies, and thus increased the outflow of capital by way of compensation payments to foreign corporations. 1963 was an altogether bad year: productivity down, unemployment at 9 per cent in Buenos

Aires and heavier in some other areas. This was an unfortunate way to inaugurate an experiment in representative democracy. A reputation for economic incompetence hung over President Illia, even though economic performance from late 1963 until the overthrow of the Radical government in June 1966 was better in terms of growth of the gross internal product than at any time since 1950 and was just as good as what would be achieved while Krieger Vasena was President Onganía's Minister of Economy from 1967 to 1970.

If, contrary to the facts, President Illia's government was popularly believed to be incompetent, the regime of General Onganía which followed achieved real incompetence. Growth did not actually cease and decline set in, but they almost did. At the end of 1966 President Onganía fired his economic advisers, and installed Adelberto Krieger Vasena as Minister of Economy. Krieger believed that the central defects of the Argentine economy were inflation and the superabundance of unproductive employments in which there was no correspondence between the output of utilities and the payment of income. Assuming that he would be firmly supported politically by President Onganía, Krieger devalued the peso severely, so that the parallel or black market disappeared. The new rate was 350 to the US dollar compared with a parallel market rate on the eve of the devaluation of 280 to the US dollar. A new peso was issued and exchanged for old pesos at the rate of one for 100. This was declared to be the last devaluation there would ever be.

For political as well as economic reasons Krieger refused to allow the revaluation of the peso to operate to the advantage of the agriculture and ranching interests. He placed a 25 per cent tax on all 'traditional' exports. On the other hand, he cut tariffs on manufactured goods, and declared the necessity for Argentine manufacturers to become competitive in international markets as well as in the Argentine market. In order to create opportunities for productive work and to absorb the underproductive workers on the railways, in the bureaucracy and in industry, he launched a large capital investment programme which aimed principally at improving the production of elec-

trical energy. By 1968 economic growth was back to the rate
achieved under President Illia. If a military regime could do as
well as a democratically elected regime, it was hoped that it
might do even better. This proved not to be the case. The
political uproar and violence under the government of Onganía
was much worse than it had been under President Illia. Super-
markets financed by foreign capital were fire-bombed. Trade
union leaders were assassinated. An ex-president of the Republic
was kidnapped and murdered. Students demonstrated and
workers struck. Signs of inflation began once more to manifest
themselves and a parallel or black market in pesos developed
once again. The soldiers became disenchanted, not with themselves, but with their man in the Casa Rosada. Onganía was
sacked. An officer with experience in public relations was sum-
moned from the Argentine Embassy in Washington, and was
made President. A new team of economic policy-makers was
installed. The peso was again devalued. Inflation followed.
There was more uproar. The President was sacked. The com-
mander-in-chief of the army took over the presidency. New
economic advisers were conscripted into the Ministry of
Finance and the Central Bank. The growth rate fell from 4·8
per cent in 1970 to 3·8 per cent in 1971, and the figures for the
first half of 1972 suggest a further fall. The rate of inflation was
40 per cent in 1971 and in the first quarter of 1972 the cost of
living index was double the rate of growth of the previous year.
For the first time since the crisis of 1951 the balance of payments on commodity account was adverse, and by a sum of US
$100,000,000. Reserves of gold and foreign exchange had
fallen from approximately US $700,000,000 in 1970 to
230,000,000 in February 1972.[21]

If the Argentine armed forces were merely a negative factor
in the economy, fastened like leeches on the body and feeding on
the bloodstream of the economically active population whose
work and management produce the goods and services of
society, the harm they do might be limited. But this is not the
case. The public sector now 'belongs' to the armed forces, and
the private sector is obliged to provide jobs and income opportunities for officers. Over 8,000 officers hold posts in the

management of industry. The railways are the province of an army group. The state air lines are a satrapy of the air force officers. The merchant marine belongs to naval officers. Because in the past General Mosconi managed the state petroleum company in its infancy with some success, it is believed, against all the evidence, that officers know something about business, and are capable of efficiently producing goods and services. If occasionally one does display some business capacity, this tends to obscure the fact that officers as a class are economically incompetent, and that their control of enterprises is one of the obstacles to economic development. The steel industry provides a deplorable example. In 1965 the National Plan fixed a production target of 4,000,000 tons of steel. To achieve the goal of independence in steel, it was assumed that growth would depend upon the development of at least three integrated steel plants: one owned and controlled by SOMISA, a mixed enterprise in which the state holds a controlling interest and private investors a minority share. The other two plants would be built by private enterprises: Propulsora and Acindar. After the military men got direct control of the government the conception of competition among steel enterprises changed. SOMISA was given the right to obtain foreign exchange at the rate of 5 new pesos to the US dollar; the others were obliged to pay 7·5 pesos for their dollars. Permits were held up in the case of the private firms. The result: in 1970 the target of 4,000,000 tons was 2,300,000 tons short of achievement.

Another example is provided in the electricity industry. Ing. Jorge Sabato was installed as President of SEGBA, the state-owned electricity generating enterprise which shares the market for electricity in Buenos Aires with a private firm owned by foreign and Argentine capital. He found that SEGBA was running deep in deficit. By the winter of 1971 losses were US $250,000 a day, and the union demanded and was granted a 29 per cent wage increase. In order to create a balance of power in the enterprises out of which some match between pricing policy and wage policy might emerge, Sabato proposed a scheme of joint ownership and control by the workers and the consumers. This sounded like common sense, but it had a fatal flaw: ownership and control by workers and consumers would mean the end of control by the military men. Sabato was immediately sacked, and an officer took his place.

Political instability and erratic economic growth have produced changes in the pattern of immigration and emigration. European immigration into Argentina has begun to fall off, and immigration from Paraguay, Chile, Peru and Bolivia has begun to grow. In 1963, for example, this bad year economically showed a net outflow of Italians, a zero movement of Germans and a net inflow of Spaniards of only 2,300.[22] On the other hand, immigration from Paraguay, Bolivia and Chile increased markedly, and the visible evidence suggests that the immigration of Indo-Americans from the limitrophe countries is greatly in excess of the official returns. One informal guess is that there are more Paraguayans in Argentina than in Paraguay.[23] A disturbing feature of the movement of people is the outflow of Argentines from Argentina. A social scientist, Enrique Otieza, has studied this development and has found that the Argentine emigrants are primarily educated, technically skilled men and women, and that their exodus fluctuates inversely with rates of economic growth. The fact is that economic disorder and bad government are changing the Argentine community from one predominantly European in character into one more and more poor, unskilled and Indo-American.

Contrary to conventional beliefs based on the experience of the nineteenth and early twentieth centuries, political disorder and bad economic management have not deterred the growth of foreign interests in Argentina. Military rhetoric about national independence, ecclesiastical rhetoric about the poor, and radical student and intellectual rhetoric about imperialism have been bad for business and for the political economy of the country, but they have been worse for Argentine business in Argentina than for foreign business in Argentina. This is understandable. Only the most powerful multi-national corporations have the means of surviving in the anti-capitalist atmosphere which has grown steadily since the officers' *coup* in 1943. Uncertainty of expectations, socialist-nationalist demagogy, inflation, the administrative sadism of state agencies and fraud have eroded the local spirit of enterprise and willingness to invest in productive undertakings of a complex and permanent character and a purely Argentine locale. The strategy of the speculator—to get in and get out with a quick large profit—and the strategy of the timid conservative—to accumulate tradeable assets like land, gold and foreign holdings—have come to dominate Argentine economic and commercial life. Large foreign firms are less touched by the uncertainties and hostility which generate fear and discouragement among those who have no homeland but Argentina. The result is that American investment, for example, has grown faster during the 1960s in Argentina than in any Latin American country except Panama, and much faster than in Mexico, Brazil and Venezuela which are popularly regarded as the darlings of American business. In 1957 US direct investment accounted for 2·2 per cent of the Argentine gross domestic product; in 1966 the percentage was 3·5. By 1970 total American direct investment was estimated at $1,285 million and was growing at a rate of 5 per cent per annum. It amounted to roughly 50 per cent of all foreign investment. British investment was 10 per cent of the total foreign investment, and the French, Germans, Dutch, Spaniards and Italians held most of the remainder. In 1966 foreign industrial firms produced 15·1 per cent of Argentine industrial output, and accounted for 40 per cent of Argentine industrial exports.[24]

A critical focal point of bad government during the 1950s and 1960s has been the budget. The International Monetary Fund has paid major attention to the budget in determining attitudes towards Argentina. While the budgets have been generally in deficit for many years, these deficits have not been phenomenally large. During the years 1965–70 inclusive the total deficit was only 15 per cent of revenue: a percentage which most economies can carry through public borrowing. The serious feature is the reason for the deficits. A heavy percentage of the national revenue is devoted to making good the losses on public enterprises and the payment of subsidies to private enterprises. This is but another way of saying that the state is paying the losses of private as well as public productive organisations. The national budget is unbalanced because the budgets of many economic enterprises are unbalanced. In other words, the outputs of goods and services by these enterprises do not cover their wage bills, their depreciation, their reserves for expansion and their administrative costs. If we assume that the art of management is at least to match output with input, and that bad management is the persistent failure to achieve this minimal match, then it is apparent that the Argentine fiscal system has become a major agency in reinforcing bad management. If the whole system works erratically and if in some instances it actually works backwards, this is because too many of the cogs in the machine are running backwards.

The soldier-politicians of Argentina are not much concerned with the supply of money, except to believe that there is never enough of it. Some of the bankers and economists who advise them have, however, been so concerned, and have believed that the supply of money, quasi-money and credit are basic factors in inflation. Credit restriction in particular has been attempted on several occasions since 1955 in an effort to stabilise prices and reduce the pressures all round for more and more of everything in the economy. It has been observed, however, that credit restriction in the Argentine situation does not reduce demand directly; it creates unemployment, reduces production and then reduces consumption. The industrial employer who cannot obtain credit or is forced to seek it outside the banking system at inflationary rates of interest is obliged not to pay wages and/or outstanding accounts and is finally forced to lay off his work force and reduce or cease production. The private employee is more adversely affected than the public employer or the multinational firm with reserves of cash or credit to fall back on.[2] The state-owned enterprises with their access to public money and credit and the multi-national enterprises with their resources of credit are able to give way to the pressure of their own organised employees for higher wages to meet inflation. The fate of the employees of private firms is unemployment or short time. The observable contradictions of the Argentine economy—spare capacity and under-used industrial plant, over-used and worn-out equipment, large wage increases and unemployment exceedingly low prices in some industries such as electricity generation and very high prices in others such as motor vehicles, negative rates of interest and high profits—are thus explicable but indefensible.

Notes to this chapter are on pp 197–8

By way of a conclusion

There is an Argentine joke which goes like this. The US Government's Space Agency planned a manned flight to Venus, but could find no American to undertake this assignment. The authorities decided to advertise internationally. Three men applied: an Italian, a Frenchman and an Argentine.

The Italian was examined first and found to be satisfactory: healthy, intelligent, brave and technically proficient. He was asked how much he required by way of pay. He replied: 'A million dollars.'

The Frenchman was found to be equally satisfactory, but when asked about pay he replied: 'Two million dollars.' He was then asked to explain why he wanted twice what the Italian had asked. The Frenchman said: 'Like the Italian I want one million as compensation for the ardours of training, my technical expertise and the dangers of the job. I also want a million to enjoy life before I leave, and to provide for my family and friends.'

The Argentine was then examined, found in every way satisfactory and asked about his pay. He replied that he wanted three million dollars.

'But why?' asked the Americans. 'An Italian will do the job for a million. A Frenchman wants two million. Here you are. You want three million. Why?'

'It is simple', replied the Argentine, 'there is a million fo you, a million for me, and we send the Italian. I'll throw in the launching site free.'

This joke presents a paradigm of Argentine economic history in so far as it relates to the distribution of the fruits of work. The possessors of Argentine resources have agreed with the possessors of capital to split the output of society three ways: a share for you, a share for me and a share for the workers. From the revolution which established the political independence of the Republic until the epoch of intellectual questioning which antedated the great depression of the 1930s by a few years, it was believed under the guise of various doctrines that the distribution of the fruits of work among those with the political control of resources, the control of capital and the power to work was a 'natural' arrangement susceptible to natural laws, which could not be broken with impunity. The laws of economics were stern laws which covered both production and distribution, and to these laws were attributed an almost sacred character. Little notice was taken of the propositions advanced as early as 1848 by one of the central presenters of economics as a science, J. S. Mill, that, while the laws of production partake of the nature of physical laws, the laws of distribution have no such character and are the product of political and institutional arrangements open to question and amendment.

Until the great depression of the 1930s there was a sense in which the Argentine economy was a natural one. Some may have questioned the moral values of Argentine life and the dominating motives of its participants, but the interests of the several parties did run parallel inasmuch as the world market absorbed more and more Argentine produce at prices which were more often than not favourable in terms of the power to purchase with the returns from their sale; and inasmuch as more and more workers would come from Europe to work in Argentina; and inasmuch as more and more capitalists would lay out the means of buying labour power and the tools of production; and inasmuch as the landowners and their governments were willing and indeed anxious to allow the use of their resources. This parallelism of interest accounts for the success

of the economy from the Baring crisis to the great depression
and for the failure of European ideologies and activists to get any
grip on the Argentine community. Some sociologists have
argued that the European immigrants imported European ideas
of socialism, anarchism and communism, ie European notions
of the distribution of wealth, and that these notions have been
eroded by time and that a new generation of 'real' Argentines
has evolved 'authentic' native responses. The truth is otherwise.
European notions about improved or ideal systems of distribution were eroded by the Argentine reality long before the
Socialists ceased speaking German and the anarchists Italian.
The Argentine Socialists of the twentieth century were free
traders, hard-money men and opponents of artificial industrialisation behind tariff walls as much as the landlords and
cattlemen and foreign capitalists. These views were not the
product of treachery to the working class nor did they weaken
the struggle of the Socialists to improve the conditions of the
people, to end the injustices and to reform the evils of capitalist
society.

The world crisis of capitalist society which commenced with
World War I and found its acutest economic expression in the
great depression impaired the parallelism of interest among the
major participants in the Argentine economy, and accordingly
raised fundamental questions concerning distribution of the
fruits of labour. The raising of questions did not necessarily
mean the production of answers. This is evident enough in
Argentina today.

Until the collapse of international prices of primary products
in the 1930s, the wealth generated by their sale was distributed
in a way which masked the reality of the agropecuarian industry. Argentine agriculture and ranching are not and never
have been manpower-intensive. The wealth of Argentine landlords has never come from skimming off the surpluses of a
numerous peasantry working the fields and pastures to provide
a subsistence for themselves. Their wealth has come from economic rent: the payments made to them by capitalists engaged
in cereal or meat production. Many of the landlords were
themselves active capitalist farmers and ranchers and as such

employers of labour. Their share of income was both economic rent and profits on capital.

In an economy based on this kind of productive activity and this form of income distribution, the creation of economic opportunities for the majority who did not work on the land depended upon two factors: the spending of the wealthy classes on their private and public activities, pleasures, luxuries and spiritual and cultural interests, and the provision of goods and services for those employed in agriculture and ranching. This explains the nature of Argentine activity in the golden age, elements of which are still present in Argentina, ie a sparsely peopled countryside productive of immense wealth, and great cities full of manpower-intensive industries and services providing an extensive range of luxurious craft products and personal services.

Since World War I conceptions of luxury have changed, and since the great depression the means of satisfying them have changed and diminished. The demand for opportunities to acquire income is the driving force of any economy at any time. In Argentina the wealth of the landlords and the requirements of the agricultural and ranching industries have become increasingly inadequate as a means of creating opportunities to acquire income. The Argentines might have stuck to agriculture and ranching, as the Spaniards did in the seventeenth century, and worked out a 'solution' of the 'income opportunity problem' by turning the nation into a community of soldiers, pensioners, monks, nuns, bureaucrats and beggars. There has been, and still is, a tendency in this direction, but on balance the more sophisticated solution of industrialisation has been put in train as a means of creating jobs. So far this solution has worked, but not quite as well as expected, and it cannot be accounted a successful solution until Argentine industry exhibits a capacity to 'stand on its own feet', ie to produce as much as it consumes, particularly in world markets. There are no reasons why success so defined cannot be achieved, and there are some signs that this may happen yet. But the 'Spanish solution' is still a possibility, too.

That the Spaniards have themselves abandoned the tradi-

tional Spanish solution, and since the civil war have begun to
exhibit the character of a modern industrial state, holds a considerable attraction for some Argentines. 'Let us', they say in
their private gatherings after they have laid aside the pam-
phlets of Opus Dei, 'have a strong Catholic, Spanish type of
government like that of the Caudillo, and all will be well.' But
will it? The Argentines only speak Spanish. They are not
Spaniards. In any case, attempts at strong government have
been tried, and they have failed. Governments must, of course,
be strong, but they must also be intelligent. For a long time
now the combination of strength and intelligence has eluded
the Argentines.

The issue in Argentina is not between an internationally
oriented, *laissez faire* capitalism and a nationally autonomous
semi-Socialist economy planned and directed by a strong
government. From first to last government has played a deter-
minant role in the Argentine economy, and political change has
established the scope and direction of economic change and
growth. From first to last the Argentine economy has been
internationally oriented. Resources and location dictate that
this should be so. From first to last the products of work have
not been distributed solely to the active participants in the
economic process, whether capitalists *and* workers or capitalists
or workers. The brute facts of politics have fixed this. And a
final negative is this. Argentina is not part of the Third World
of poverty and under-development requiring some special
attention and assistance.

It is easy to say what Argentina is not. But what is it as an
economic type? Like its erstwhile principal trading partner,
Great Britain, Argentina is a stranded economic dinosaur from
the epoch before the great world wars of the twentieth century.
They know they 'ain't what they used to be'. This worries
them, but they have not adjusted wholly to the present, let
alone found a future. Illusion and confusion have permeated
all sections of society from top to bottom. The poor think the
rich are too rich, and the rich think the poor are too powerful
and well-off. The reality is otherwise. Without being in a steady
state, Argentina is near stagnation. There is tremendous energy

in society, but this is as likely to produce spontaneous combustion as anything else. It would be a bold man who would prescribe for Argentina, but economists, sociologists and experts from the International Monetary Fund are constantly doing so. It is said that wealth disorientates communities, and that societies, like individuals, find it hard to be rich and sane at the same time. Perhaps Argentina is finding a solution to this problem by becoming poor, and by the most modern of means, industrialisation.

Notes

Chapter 1 THE COLONIAL ECONOMY (pp 11–21)

1 Horacio Giberti, *Historia económica de la ganaderia Argentina* (Buenos Aires, 1954), p 43

2 Peter H. Smith, *Politics and beef in Argentina: patterns of conflict and change* (New York: Columbia UP, 1969), p 45

Chapter 2 FROM THE REVOLUTION TO ROSAS (pp 22–36)

1 José M. Mariluz Urquijo, *Estado e industria 1810–62* (Buenos Aires, 1969), p 67

2 José Panettieri, *Inmigración en la Argentina* (Buenos Aires, 1970) p 17

3 Efrain U. Bischoff, *Historia de la provincia de Córdoba* (Córdoba, 1969), I, 257–8, 269

4 Bischoff, *Córdoba*, I, 303–4

Chapter 3 A POLICY FOR NATIONAL DEVELOPMENT (pp 37–52)

1 Ernesto J. A. Maeder, *Evolución demográfica argentina desde 1810 a 1869* (Buenos Aires, 1969), passim

2 Juan Bialet-Massé, *El estado de las clases obreros Argentina a commienzos del siglo*, ed Luis A. Despontin (Córdoba, 1968)

3 Gino Germani, *Estructura social de la Argentina* (Buenos Aires, 1955), passim

4 José C. Chiaramonte, 'Le crisis de 1866 y el protectionisimo Argentina de la decada del 1870' in Torcuato S. di Tella y Tulio Halperín Donghi, *Los Argentinos: los fragmentos del poder* (Buenos Aires, 1969), pp 171–215

5 Chiaramonte, 'Le crisis de 1866', p 208

Chapter *4* TWO DECADES OF DEVELOPMENT, 1870–1890 (pp 53–72)

1 Eduardo Zalduendo, *Las inversiones britanícas para la promoción y desarrollo de ferrocarriles en el siglo XIX* (Buenos Aires, 1969), II, Appendix 15, with some revisions

2 Aníbal B. Arcondo, *La agricultura en Córdoba, 1870–1880* (Córdoba, 1965), p 40

3 Carl C. Taylor, *Rural life in Argentina* (Baton Rouge: Louisiana State UP, 1948), pp 197ff

4 Vicente Vásquez-Presedo, *El caso argentino: migracion de factores, comercio exterior y desarrollo, 1875–1914* (Buenos Aires, 1971), p 140

5 Ezequiel Gallo, 'Agricultural colonization and society in Argentina: the province of Santa Fe' (Oxford University DPhil thesis, 1970), p 233

6 Gallo, 'Agricultural colonization', p 312

7 Vásquez-Presedo, *El caso argentino*, pp 16, 149; James R. Scobie, *Revolution on the Pampas: a social history of Argentine wheat, 1860–1910* (Austin: University of Texas Press, 1964), p 170

Chapter *5* THE BARING CRISIS AND AFTER, 1890–1899 (pp 73–86)

1 Alec G. Ford, *The gold standard 1880–1914: Britain and Argentina* (Oxford: Clarendon Press, 1962), p 148

2 Vásquez-Presedo, *El caso argentino*, p 92

3 Scobie, *Revolution on the Pampas*, p 170

4 Giberti, *Historia económica de la ganaderia Argentina*, p 187

5 Gino Miniati (ed), *La industralización y el ahorro de devisas en la Argentina* (Buenos Aires, 1959), p 43

6 John H. Williams, *Argentine international trade under inconvertible paper money, 1880–1900* (Cambridge, Mass: Harvard UP, 1920), p 197

7 Alec G. Ford, 'Argentina and the Baring crisis of 1890', *Oxford Economic Papers*, VIII (1956), 135

8 Williams, *Argentine international trade*, p 119

9 Ibid

10 Ford, 'Argentina and the Baring crisis', 144

11 Ford, *Gold standard*, p 139

12 Henry S. Ferns, *Britain and Argentina in the nineteenth century* (Oxford: Clarendon Press, 1960), pp 464–77

13 Ford, *Gold standard*, p 144

14 Alec G. Ford, 'Export price indices for the Argentine Republic, 1881–1894', *Inter-American Economic Affairs*, IX, no 2 (1955), 45
15 Vásquez-Presedo, *El caso argentino*, p 149
16 Ford, *Gold standard*, p 139
17 Williams, *Argentine international trade*, pp 155–62; Ford, *Gold standard*, pp 95–199
18 Ricardo M. Ortiz, *Historia económica de la Argentina, 1850–1930*, II (2nd ed, Buenos Aires, 1964), p 296

Chapter 6 THE GOLDEN AGE, 1899–1929 (pp 87–115)
1 Based on data in United Nations, *El desarrollo económico de la Argentina* (Mexico, 1959), I, 36, 113, and Carlos F. Díaz Alejandro, *Essays in the economic history of the Argentine Republic* (New Haven: Yale UP, 1970), pp 30, 43
2 Díaz Alejandro, *Essays*, pp 8, 10
3 United Nations, *El desarrollo económico*, I, 110
4 Associacion de Fabricas de Automotores, *Industria Automotriz Argentina* (Buenos Aires, 1970), p 22
5 Colin Clark, *The conditions of economic progress* (Macmillan, 1940), p 2
6 Díaz Alejandro, *Essays*, p 8
7 Based on data in Díaz Alejandro, *Essays*, p 440, and Ortiz, *Historia económica de la Argentina*, II, 232
8 United Nations, *El desarrollo económico*, II, 29
9 Díaz Alejandro, *Essays*, pp 428–9
10 Jacinto Oddone, *La burguesía terrateniente Argentina* (Buenos Aires, 1967), pp 185–6
11 Oddone, *La burguesía terrateniente Argentina*, pp 251–2
12 Taylor, *Rural life in Argentina*, pp 197ff and passim
13 United Nations, *El desarrollo económico*, II, 12
14 Taylor, *Rural life in Argentina*, p 108
15 Díaz Alejandro, *Essays*, p 160
16 Based on Díaz Alejandro, *Essays*, pp 436, 440, and United Nations, *El desarrollo económico*, II, 21
17 Ortiz, *Historia económica de la Argentina*, II, 63
18 Vásquez-Presedo, *El caso argentino*, p 149
19 Simon G. Hanson, *Argentine meat and the British market: chapters in the history of the Argentine meat industry* (Stanford UP, 1937), p 129
20 Smith, *Politics and beef*, p 46
21 Taylor, *Rural life in Argentina*, pp 49, 51

22 United Nations, *El desarrollo económico*, II, 37
23 George Wythe, *Industry in Latin America* (2nd ed, New York, 1949), p 90
24 Based on Díaz Alejandro, *Essays*, p 212, and *Censo industrial, 1914*
25 Vásquez-Presedo, *El caso argentino*, p 202
26 Díaz Alejandro, *Essays*, p 210
27 Adolfo Dorfman, *Historia de la industria Argentina* (Buenos Aires, 1970), p 352
28 Quoted in Dorfman, *Historia de la industria Argentina*, p 358
29 Wythe, *Industry in Latin America*, p 105
30 Díaz Alejandro, *Essays*, p 215
31 eg Leopoldo Portnoy, *La realidad Argentina en el siglo XIX* (Mexico, 1961); Ortiz, *Historia económica de la Argentina*; Felix J. Weil, *The Argentine riddle* (New York, 1944); Raúl Scalabrini Ortiz, *Política británica en el Rio de la Plata* (Buenos Aires, 1929)
32 Díaz Alejandro, *Essays*, pp 295–300
33 Samuel L. Baily, *Nationalism and organised labour in Argentina 1890–1955* (New Brunswick, NY: Rutgers UP, 1967), p 70
34 *Report of the British Economic Mission to Argentina, Brazil and Uruguay* (London, 1930), pp 15–16
35 Thomas C. Cochran and Ruben E. Reina, *Entrepreneurship in Argentine culture: Torcuato di Tella and SIAM [Sociedad Industrial Americana Maquinarias]* (Philadelphia, 1962), passim
36 Díaz Alejandro, *Essays*, p 35
37 United Nations, *El desarrollo económico*, I, 79
38 Smith, *Politics and beef*, p 60
39 Plácido Grela, *El grito de Alcorta: historia de la rebelión campesina de 1912* (Rosario, 1958), pp 72–4

Chapter 7 THE RESPONSE TO CRISIS, 1929–1939 (pp 116–38)

1 Díaz Alejandro, *Essays*, p 438
2 United Nations, *El desarrollo económico*, I, 20
3 Díaz Alejandro, *Essays*, p 71
4 Walter M. Beveraggi Allende, *El servicio del capital extranjero y el control de cambios: la experiencia argentina de 1900 a 1943* (Mexico, 1954), p 156
5 His Majesty's Stationery Office (HMSO), *Argentina: review of commercial conditions* (London, 1945), p 4
6 Beveraggi Allende, *El servicio del capital*, p 166

7   Virgil Salera, *Exchange control and the Argentine market* (New York: Columbia UP, 1941), p 42
8   Díaz Alejandro, *Essays*, p 475
9   Vernon L. Phelps, *The international economic position of Argentina* (Philadelphia: University of Pennsylvania Press, 1938), p 217
10   Phelps, *The international economic position of Argentina*, pp 206–9
11   *Convention between the government of the United Kingdom and the government of the Argentine Republic relating to trade and commerce* (HMSO, Accounts and Papers 1933–4, Cmd 4492)
12   HMSO, *Argentina: review of economic conditions*, p 11
13   Díaz Alejandro, *Essays*, p 461
14   Ibid, p 95
15   US Government, Office of Economic Warfare, *Argentina* (Washington, 1944), pp 100, 110
16   Roger Gravil, 'State intervention in Argentina's export trade between the wars', *Journal of Latin American Studies*, II (1970), 150
17   Asociacíon de Fabricas de Automotores, *Industria automotriz Argentina*, p 22
18   Phelps, *The international economic position of Argentina*, p 97
19   Díaz Alejandro, *Essays*, p 424
20   Aldo Ferrer, *The Argentine economy* (Berkeley: University of California Press, 1967), p 227
21   Díaz Alejandro, *Essays*, p 95
22   Ibid, p 458
23   Ibid, p 514
24   United Nations, *El desarrollo económico*, I, 114
25   Ministerio de Hacienda, *Estadistica industrial de 1939* (Buenos Aires, 1942)
26   Díaz Alejandro, *Essays*, p 504
27   Salera, *Exchange control*, p 118
28   Evidence supplied to the author by a former officer of YPF.
29   Díaz Alejandro, *Essays*, p 428
30   United Nations, *El desarrollo económico*, I, 112
31   Ibid, 114
32   T. Amadeo, *Boletin del Museo Social Argentino*, xxxvi (1948)
33   Díaz Alejandro, *Essays*, p 427
34   Taylor, *Rural life in Argentina*, p 297
35   United Nations, *El desarrollo económico*, II, 37
36   US Bureau of Labour Statistics, *Labour conditions in Latin America* (1940)

Chapter 8 THE RESPONSE TO WAR AND CHANGE, 1940–1955 (pp 139–65)

1 Díaz Alejandro, *Essays*, p 477
2 Ibid, pp 472–3
3 HMSO, *Argentina: review of commercial conditions*, p 38
4 Díaz Alejandro, *Essays*, p 103
5 United Nations, *El desarrollo económico*, I, 20
6 Ibid, p 124
7 Díaz Alejandro, *Essays*, p 124
8 United Nations, *El desarrollo económico*, I, 80–2
9 Ibid., p 71
10 Díaz Alejandro, *Essays*, p 425
11 United Nations, *El desarrollo económico*, II, 10
12 Ibid, 110
13 Ibid, 82
14 Ibid, I, 83
15 Díaz Alejandro, *Essays*, p 497
16 Ibid, p 488
17 Ibid, pp 527–8
18 United Nations, *El desarrollo económico*, II, 172
19 José L. de Imaz, *Los que mandan* (Buenos Aires, 1965), p 216
20 Díaz Alejandro, *Essays*, p 329

Chapter 9 INDUSTRIALISATION, 1955–1971 (pp 166–85)

1 Centro de Industriales Siderúrgicos, *La siderurgía argentina en 1968* (Buenos Aires, 1968); *Boletin de Estadistica* (Buenos Aires, 1971)
2 *Estadistica Minera de la Republica Argentina* (Buenos Aires, 1967); *Boletin de Estadistica*, 1961–71
3 Asociación de Fabricas de Automotores, *Industria automotriz Argentina 1970* (Buenos Aires, 1971)
4 United Nations, *World energy supplies* (various years); *Boletin de Estadistica*
5 Banco Central de la Republic Argentina, *Origen del producto y distribucion del ingreso años, 1950–69* (Buenos Aires, 1971)
6 Ecos Diarios, Nicochea, 19 March 1972, quoted in *The Review of the River Plate*, 20 April 1972
7 *The Review of the River Plate*, 21 May 1972
8 Richard D. Mallon, 'Exchange policy', in Gustav F. Papanek (ed), *Development policy: theory and practice* (Cambridge, Mass, 1966), p 183

9   Mallon, 'Exchange policy', pp 202–4

10 Díaz Alejandro, *Essays*, pp 333–50, 381

11 Julio Broner y Daniel E. Larriqueta, *La revolucion industrial argentina* (Buenos Aires, 1969), chapter III, and Asociación de Fabricas de Automotores, *Industria automotriz Argentina 1970*, p 17

12 Asociación de Fabricas de Automotores, *Informe economico, 1969*, privately printed

13 Díaz Alejandro, *Essays*, pp 472–3

14 *Guia Agropecuaria Argentina*, 1965–6, p 645

15 Díaz Alejandro, *Essays*, p 168

16 Mallon, 'Exchange policy', p 185

17 Broner y Larriqueta, *La revolucion industrial*, chapter II

18 *Guia Agropecuaria Argentina*, 1965–6, p 647

19 Pan American Union, Inter-American Committee for Agricultural Development, *Land tenure conditions and socio-economic development of the agricultural sector, Argentina* (Washington, 1965), p 42

20 Ministerio de Hacienda y Finanzos, *Informe economico* (1971), 86

21 *The Banker*, June 1972, 483

22 *Boletin de Estadistica* (1964), 46–7

23 Made by an Argentine Ambassador to Paraguay in conversation with the author

24 John H. Dunning, 'Investment in Argentina', *The Banker*, CXXII (1972), 735–40

25 Geoffrey Maynard and Willy van Rijckeghem, 'Stabilization policy in an inflationary economy' in Papanek (ed), *Development policy: theory and practice*, p 210

Bibliography

Alemann, Roberto T. *Curso de política económia Argentina* (Buenos Aires, 1970)

Alexander, Robert J. *An introduction to Argentina* (1969)

Alsina, Juan A. *La inmigración en el primer siglo de la independencia* (Buenos Aires, 1910)

Arcondo, Aníbal B. *La agricultura en Córdoba, 1870–1880* (Córdoba, 1965)

Asociación de Fabricas de Automotores. *Industria Automotriz Argentina 1970* (Buenos Aires, 1971)

Avellaneda, Nicholás. *Estudio sobre las leyes de tierras públicas* (Buenos Aires, 1915)

Azara, Félix de. *Memoria sobre el estado rural del Río de la Plata y otros informes* (Buenos Aires, 1943)

Bagú, Sergio. *Evolución histórica de la estratificación social en la Argentina* (Caracas, 1969)

——. *El plan económico del grupo Rivadaviano 1821–1827* (Buenos Aires, 1966)

Baily, Samuel L. *Labor, nationalism and politics in Argentina* (New Brunswick, NJ, 1967)

Banco Central de la Republica Argentina, *Boletin Estadistica*, various years with supplements on topics such as the balance of payments, estimates of GNP, etc

——. *Origen del producto y distribucion del ingreso, años 1950–69* (Buenos Aires, 1971)

Barager, Joseph R. (ed). *Why Perón came to power: the background of Peronism in Argentina* (New York, 1968)

Beveraggi Allende, Walter M. *El servicio del capital extranjero y el control de cambios: la experiencia argentina de 1900 a 1943* (Mexico 1954)

Bialet-Massé, Juan. *El estado de las clases obreras argentinas a comienzos del siglo*, ed Despontin, Lavis A. (Córdoba, 1968)

Bischoff, Efrain U. *Historia de la provincia de Córdoba* (Córdoba, 1970)

Bliss, Horacio W. *Del virreinato a Rosas: ensayo di historia económica Argentina, 1776–1829* (Tucumán, 1959)

Brodersohn, Mario S. (ed). *Estrategias de industrialización para la Argentina* (Buenos Aires, 1970)

Broner, Daniel E. y Larriqueta, Julio. *La revolución industrial argentina*, (Buenos Aires, 1969)

Bryce, James B. *South America: observations and impressions* (New York and London, 1912)

Bunge, Alejandro E. *La economía argentina* (Buenos Aires, 1928–30)

Burgin, Miron. *The economic aspects of Argentine federalism, 1820–1852* (Cambridge, Mass, 1946)

Cárcano, Miguel A. *Evolución histórica del régimen de la tierra publica, 1810–1916* (Buenos Aires, 1925)

Carretero, Andrés M. *Los Anchorena: politica y negocios en el siglo XIX* (Buenos Aires, 1970)

Centro de Industriales Siderúrgicos. *La siderurgía argentina en 1968* (Buenos Aires, 1969)

Chambers, Edward J. 'Some factors in the deterioration of Argentina's external position, 1946–1951', *Inter-American Economic Affairs*, VIII, no 3 (1954), 27–62

Chiaramonte, José C. *Nacionalismo y liberalismo económicos en Argentina 1860–1880* (Buenos Aires, 1971)

Cochran, Thomas C. and Reina, Ruben E. *Entrepreneurship in Argentine culture: Torcuato di Tella and SIAM [Sociedad Industrial Americana Maquinarias]* (Philadelphia, 1962)

Coni, Emilio A. *El gaucho: Argentina, Brasil, Uruguay* (Buenos Aires, 1945)

——. *Historia de los vaquerías del Río de la Plata, 1555–1750* (Madrid, 1930)

——. *La verdad sobre la enfiteusis de Rivadavia* (Buenos Aires, 1927)

Comadran Ruiz, J. *Evolución demografica argentina durante el períodc hispano, 1535–1810* (Buenos Aires, 1969)

Consejo Nacional de Desarrollo, *Plan nacional de desarrollo, 1965–196ς* (Buenos Aires, 1965)

Convention between the government of the United Kingdom and the governmen of the Argentine Republic relating to trade and commerce (HMSO Accounts and Papers 1933–34, Cmd 4492)

Cornblit, Oscar, 'Inmigrantes y empresarios en la politica Argentina', *Desarrollo Economico*, VI, No 24 (1967)

Conde, Roberto Cortes y Gallo, Ezequiel, *La formacion de la Argentina moderno* (Buenos Aires, 1967)

Cuccorese, Horacio J. *Historia de la conversión del papel moneda en Buenos Aires 1861–67* (La Plata, 1959)

——. *Historia de los ferrocarriles en la Argentina* (Buenos Aires, 1969)

Cuccorese, Horacio J. *y* Panettieri, José. *Argentina, manual de historia económia y social* (Buenos Aires, 1971)

Darwin, Charles R. *Journal of Charles Darwin, MA, naturalist to the Beagle (1832–1836)* (1839)

Denis, Pierre. *The Argentine Republic: its development and progress*, translated from French by Joseph McCabe (1922)

Díaz Alejandro, Carlos F. *Devalución de la tasa de cambio en un pais semi-industrializado: la experiencia de la Argentina 1955–1961* (Buenos Aires, 1966)

——. *Essays on the economic history of the Argentine Republic* (New Haven, Conn, 1970)

Dorfman, Adolfo, *Historia de la industria argentina* (Buenos Aires, 1942)

Dunning, John H. 'Investment in Argentina', *The Banker*, CXXII (1972), 735–40

Erickkson, J. R. 'El comportamiento de la exportación de manufacturas en la Argentina, 1951–65', *Desarrollo Económico*, IX (1970)

Eshag, Eprime and Thorp, Rosemary. 'Economic and social consequences of orthodox economic policies in Argentina in the postwar years', *Bulletin of the Oxford University Institute of Economics and Statistics*, XXVII (1965), 3–44

Felix, David, 'The dilemma of import substitution—Argentina', in Papanek, Gustav F. (ed), *Development policy: theory and practice* (Cambridge, Mass, 1968), pp 55–91

Ferns, Henry S. *Argentina* (London, 1969)

——. *Britain and Argentina in the nineteenth century* (Oxford, 1960)

Ferrer, Aldo. *The Argentine economy*, translated by Urquidi, Marjory M. (Berkeley, California, 1967)

Ferrer, Aldo and Wheelwright, Edward L. *Industrialization in Argentina and Australia: a comparative study* (mimeographed, Buenos Aires, 1966)

Fienup, Darrell F., Brannon, Russell H. and Fender, Frank A. *The agricultural development of Argentina: a policy and development perspective* (New York, 1969)

Fillol, Tomás R. *Social factors in economic development: the Argentine case* (Cambridge, Mass, 1961)

Fitte, Ernesto J. *Historia de un empréstito: La emissión de Baring Brothers en 1824* (Buenos Aires, 1962)

Ford, Alec G. 'Argentina and the Baring Crisis of 1890', *Oxford Economic Papers*, VIII (1956), 127–50

——. 'Export price indices for the Argentine Republic, 1881–1914', *Inter-American Economic Affairs*, IX, no 2 (1955), 42–54

——. *The gold standard, 1880–1914: Britain and Argentina* (Oxford, 1962)

Frigerio, Rogelio. *Crecimiento económico y democracia* (Buenos Aires, 1963)

Gallo, Ezequiel. 'Agricultural colonization and society in Argentina: the province of Santa Fe, 1870–1895' (Oxford University PhD thesis, 1970)

——. 'Agricultural expansion and industrial development in Argentina' in Carr, Raymond (ed), *Latin American affairs* (St Anthony's Papers, no 22, Oxford, 1970), pp 45–61

Germani, Gino. *Política y sociedad en una época de transición* (Buenos Aires, 1965)

Giberti, Horacio C. E. *El desarrollo agrario argentino: Estudio de la region pampeana* (Buenos Aires, 1964)

——. *Historia económica de la ganaderia Argentina* (Buenos Aires, 1954)

Gibson, Sir Herbert. *The history and present state of the sheep-breeding industry in the Argentine Republic* (Buenos Aires, 1893)

Gondra, Luis R. *Historia económica de la Republica Argentina* (Buenos Aires, 1943)

Gori, Gastón. *El pan nuestro* (Buenos Aires, 1958)

Gravil, Roger. 'State intervention in Argentina's export trade between the wars', *Journal of Latin American Studies*, II (1970), 147–73

Grela, Plácido. *El grito de Alcorta: historia de la rebelión campesina de 1912* (Rosario, 1958)

Guglialmelli, Juan E. *120 dias en el gobierno* (Buenos Aires, 1971)

Guia Agropecuaria Argentina (Buenos Aires, various years)

Hadfield, William. *Brazil and the River Plate in 1868* (1869)

Halperin Donghi, Tulio. 'La expansion ganadera en la campaña de Buenos Aires, 1810–1852', *Desarrollo Economico*, III (1963), 57–110

Hanson, Simon G. *Argentine meat and the British market: chapters in the history of the Argentine meat industry* (Stanford UP, 1938)

Harvard University Bureau for Economic Research in Latin

America. *The economic literature of Latin America* (2 vols, Cambridge, Mass, 1935–6)

Head, Sir Francis B. *Rough notes taken during some rapid journeys across the Pampas and among the Andes* (1826)

Hudson, William H. *Far away and long ago: a history of my early life* (1918)

Humphreys, Robin A. *British consular reports on the trade and politics of Latin America, 1824–1826* (Camden Society third series, LXIII, 1940)

Huret, Jules. *En Argentina: de Buenos Aires au Gran Chaco* (Paris, 1913)

——. *En Argentina: de la Plata a la Cordillère des Andes* (Paris, 1913)

Hutchinson, Thomas J. *Buenos Aires and Argentine gleanings, with extracts from a diary of Salado exploration in 1862 and 1863* (1865)

Imaz, José L. de. *Los que mandan* (Buenos Aires, 1965)

Iparraguirra, Hilda y Pianetto, Ofelia. *La organización de la clase obrerac en Córdoba, 1870–1895* (Córdoba, 1968)

James, Preston E. *Latin America* (3rd ed, New York, 1959)

Jauretche, Arturo. *El medio pelo en la sociedad Argentina: a puntes para una sociología nacional* (Buenos Aires, 1966)

Jefferson, Mark. *Peopling the Argentine pampa* (New York, 1926)

Joslin, David. *A century of banking in Latin America: to commemorate the centenary in 1962 of the Bank of England & South America Limited* (Oxford, 1963)

Katz, Jorge M. *Production functions, foreign investment and growth: a study based on the Argentine manufacturing sector, 1946–1961* (Amsterdam and London, 1969)

Latham, Wilfrid. *The states of the River Plate: their industries & commerce* (1866)

Lavardén, Manuel de. *Nuevo aspecto del comercio en el Río de la Plata,* Estudio preliminar y notas por Enrique Wedovoy (Buenos Aires, 1955)

Lawson, William R. 'Gaucho banking', *'The Bankers', Insurance Managers' and Agents' Magazine,* LI (1891), 33–52

Lynch, John. *Spanish colonial administration: 1782–1810: the intendant system in the viceroyalty of the Río de la Plata* (1958)

MacCann, William. *Two thousand miles ride through the Argentine provinces,* 2 vols (1853)

McGann, Thomas F. *Argentina: the divided land* (Princeton, NJ, 1966)

——. *Argentina: the United States and the inter-American system, 1880–1914* (Cambridge, Mass, 1957)

Maeder, Ernesto J. A. *Evolución demográfica argentina de 1810 a 1869* (Buenos Aires, 1969)

Mallon, Richard D. 'Exchange policy' in Papanek, Gustav F. (ed), *Development policy: theory and practice* (Cambridge, Mass, 1968), pp 175–206

——. 'Planning in crisis', *Journal of Political Economy*, LXXVIII (1970), 948–65

Mariluz Urquijo, José M. (ed), *Estado e industria 1810–1862* (Buenos Aires, 1969)

Marotta, Sebastián. *El movimiento sindical argentino* (Buenos Aires, 1960–70)

Martinez, Alberto B. and Lewandowski, Maurice. *The Argentine in the twentieth century* (1911)

Mayer, Jorge M. *Alberdi y su tiempo* (Buenos Aires, 1963)

Maynard, Geoffrey and Rijckegham, Willy van. 'Stabilization policy in an inflationary economy', in Papanek, Gustav F (ed), *Development policy: theory and practice* (Cambridge, Mass, 1968), pp 207–35

Miniati, Gino (ed). *Argentina económica y financiero* (Buenos Aires, 1960; 2nd ed, 1963; 3rd ed, 1971)

——. *La industrialización y el ahorra de devisas en la Argentina* (Buenos Aires, 1959)

Montoya, Alfreda J. *Historia de los saladeros argentinos* (Buenos Aires, 1956)

Moyano Llerena, Carlos. *Argentina, social y económica* (Buenos Aires, 1950)

Mulhall, Michael G. and Mulhall, Edward T. *Handbook of the River Plate, compris ingBuenos Aires, the Upper Provinces, Banda Oriental and Paraguay* (Buenos Aires, 1863 and later editions)

Oddone, Jacinto. *La burguesía terrateniente argentina* (Buenos Aires, 1967)

Olarra Jimínez, Rafael. *Evolución monetaria argentina* (Buenos Aires, 1968)

Organisation for Economic Cooperation and Development. *Education, human resources and development in Argentina* (Paris, 1967)

Ortiz, Ricardo M. *El ferrocarril en la economía argentina* (Buenos Aires, 1950)

——. *Historia económica de la Argentina, 1850–1930* (Buenos Aires, 1955)

Oteiza, Enrique. 'Emigración de profesionales, tecnicos y obreros calificados argentinos a los Estados Unidos: analisis de las fluc-

tuaciones de la emigracion bruta Julio 1950 a Junio 1970',
Desarrollo Económico, X (1971), 429–54

Palmieri, Horacio J. y Colome, R. A.. 'La industria manufactureria
en la ciudad de Córdoba', *Revista de Economia y Estadistico* (1964)

Panettieri, José. *Inmigración en la Argentina* (Buenos Aires, 1970)

———. *Los trabajodores en tiempos de la inmigración masiva en Argentina,
1870–1910* (Buenos Aires, 1967)

Parish, Sir Woodbine. *Buenos Aires and the provinces of the Rio de la
Plata* (2nd ed, 1852)

Pendle, George. *Argentina* (3rd ed, Oxford, 1963)

Peters, Harold E. *The foreign debt of the Argentine Republic* (Baltimore:
Johns Hopkins Press, 1934)

Phelps, Vernon L. *The international economic position of Argentina*
(Philadelphia, 1938)

Pinedo, Federico. *Siglo y medio de economía Argentina* (Mexico, 1961)

Portnoy, Leopoldo. *Análisis crítico de la economía argentina* (Mexico,
1961)

Potash, Robert A. *The army and politics in Argentina 1928–1945*
(Stanford UP, 1969)

Prebisch, Raúl. *Comentarios sobre el Informe preliminar* (Buenos Aires,
1955)

———. *Moneda sana o inflación incontenible* (Buenos Aires, 1956)

Quintero, Ramos, A. N. *Historia monetaria y bancaria de Argentina*
(New York, 1970)

Rennie, Isabel F. *The Argentine Republic* (New York, 1945)

Republica Argentina, Direccion Nacional de Estadistica y Censos.
Boletin de Estadistica (quarterly each year)

———, Ministerio de Haciendo y Finanzas. *Informe Económica* (Buenos
Aires, various years)

Río, Manuel E. *Los finanzas de Córdoba en los ultimos viente años, 1878–
1895* (Córdoba, 1900)

———. *Deuda pública de Córdoba* (Córdoba, 1899)

Robertson, John P. and Robertson, William P. *Letters on South
America: comprising travels on the banks of the Parana and Rio de la
Plata* (1843)

Romero, José L. *A history of Argentine political thought*, translated by
McGann, Thomas F. (Stanford UP, 1963)

Rumbold, Sir Horace. *The great silver river: notes of a residence in
Buenos Aires in 1880 and 1881* (1887)

Salera, Virgil. *Exchange control and the Argentine market* (New York,
1941)

Sarmiento, Domingo F. *Life in the Argentine Republic in the days of the tyrants: or, civilization and barbarism* (New York, 1868 and 1961)

Sbarra, Noel H. *Historia del alambrado argentina* (Buenos Aires, 1964)

Scalabrini Ortiz, Raúl. *Historia de los ferrocarriles argentinos* (Buenos Aires, 1940)

——. *Política britanicá en el Rio de la Plata* (Buenos Aires, 1929; 2nd ed, 1940; 3rd ed, 1957)

Scobie, James R. *Argentina: a city and a nation* (2nd ed, New York, 1971)

——. *Buenos Aires hacia 1900* (Buenos Aires, 1971)

——. *Revolution on the Pampas: a social history of Argentine wheat 1860–1910* (Austin, Texas, 1964)

Silverman, B. 'Economic development in the Peronist epoch', *Studies in Comparative International Development*, IV (1968–9)

Smith, Peter H. *Politics and beef in Argentina: patterns of conflict and change* (New York, 1969)

Solberg, Carl E. *Immigration and nationalism: Argentina and Chile 1890–1914* (Austin: University of Texas Press for Institute of Latin American Studies, 1970)

Taylor, Carl C. *Rural life in Argentina* (Baton Rouge, Louisiana, 1948)

Tella, Guido di y Zymelman, Manuel. *Los etapas del desarrollo económico argentino* (Buenos Aires, 1967)

Tella, Torcuato S. di. *El sistema político argentino y la clase obrera* (Buenos Aires, 1964)

Tella, Torcuato S. di, Germani, Gino, *et al. Argentina, sociedad de mases* (Buenos Aires, 1965)

Tjarks, Germán O. E. *El consulado de Buenos Aires y sus proyecciones en la historia del Rio de la Plata* (Buenos Aires, 1962)

Tornquist, Ernesto. *The economic development of the Argentine Republic in the last fifty years* (Buenos Aires, 1919)

United Nations, *El desarrollo económico de la Argentina* (México, 1959)

——. *El desarrollo económico y la distribucion del ingreso en la Argentina* (New York, 1968)

——, Department of Economic Affairs. *Economic survey of Latin America, 1948* (Lake Success, 1949; see also later editions)

US Government, Office of Economic Warfare. *Argentina* (mimeographed, Washington, 1944)

Vásquez-Presedo, Vicente. *El caso argentino: migracion de factores, comercio exterior y desarrollo, 1875–1914* (Buenos Aires, 1971)

Weil, Felix J. *The Argentine riddle* (New York, 1944)

Weinberg, Felix, *et al. Florencio Varela y el 'Commercio del Plata'* (Bahia Blanca, 1970)

Williams, John H. *Argentine international trade under inconvertible paper money, 1880–1900* (Cambridge, Mass, 1920)

Winsberg, Morton D. *Colonia Barón Hirsch: a jewish agricultural colony in Argentina* (Gainesville, Florida, 1964)

Wythe, George. *Industry in Latin America* (2nd ed, New York, 1949)

Zalduendo, Eduardo. *Las inversiones británicas para la promocion y desarrollo de ferrocarriles en el siglo XIX* (mimeographed, Buenos Aires, 1968)

Zuvekas, Clarence, 'Argentine economic policy, 1958–62: the Frondizi Government's development plan', *Inter-American Economic Affairs*, XXII (1968), 45–73

Index